HOW THE EARTH WAS LOST

HOW THE EARTH WAS LOST

David Schmoller

Yellowfield Biological Surveys

2019

First Printing: 2019

ISBN 978-0-578-52042-1

Yellowfield Biological Surveys
P. O. Box 1774
Woodruff, WI 54568

Editor: David Schmoller

Unless otherwise noted, all artwork, photographs, and design: David Schmoller

www.biologicalsurveys.com

Dedication

To those who survive it.

Contents

Introduction

Geologists say that there are about seven quintillion grains of sand on earth. Astronomers say that there are about one sextillion stars in the universe. That's seven thousand times more stars than grains of sand. Maybe that's because the earth, relatively speaking, is quite small. It just seems big because it's a sphere and we are tiny. It would take about 21 million of us laid head to toe to span its circumference. An expedition around the equator seems endless. Every three years you pass a familiar looking island where the natives call you by your first name. You wonder why and keep sailing on; somewhere beyond that horizon is the west pole. Were the earth a flat rectangle, one would bump into the edge and realize that there is nothing more. Sailing any further, you would cascade over the icy rim, descending into deep space, joining thousands of screaming, skeletal, pre-Columbian sailors.

That's a lot of stars. With them, come a lot of planets. It has been estimated that there may be billions or trillions of planets in the Milky Way alone, one of ten billion galaxies in our ever-expanding universe. In fact, scientists have detected over four thousand of these exoplanets to date.

Some of the exoplanets appear to have conditions favorable for life as we know it. This suggests that there may be billions or trillions of planets in the universe with conditions favorable for life.

It has been theorized that some of that life would be intelligent. Were that the case, with billions or trillions of planets that have life potential, advanced intelligent life would be highly probable and frequent, so advanced that it would be exploring the galaxies, broadcasting static-filled greetings over electromagnetic waves, spinning through cornfields, shutting down the power grid, buzzing military jets, abducting children, eviscerating cattle, and darting off into space, making a series of right-angle turns at the speed of light.

In 1950, the renowned physicist Enrico Fermi was on lunch break at Los Alamos National Laboratory discussing the lack of evidence of intelligent extraterrestrial life with his fellow physicists. As the conversation drifted to other subjects, Fermi blurted, "But where *are* they?"[1]

Good question. Some have tried to explain Fermi's paradox, the absence of alien contact. In 1996, economist Robin Hanson proposed the *Great Filter* theory.[2] In it, he argued that the reason for the absence is the failure of life to advance past at least one of nine steps required to reach interstellar exploration. That is to say, at least one of the steps must be highly improbable. And the argument seems to be that the last step, interstellar exploration, is the highly improbable step and it is highly probable that it has been impeded by anthropogenic catastrophe, where humanity self-destructs, civilization hangs itself. Some may argue that it is highly likely that this would make a great science-fiction film.

Speaking of which, one year after Fermi's outburst, a flying saucer containing an advanced, plant-like alien crashed in the arctic. The alien went on a rampage, killing animals and humans and had started replicating just before it was doused with kerosene and electrocuted, after which Douglas Spencer broadcast an urgent warning to the world, telling everybody to "keep watching the skies."[3] In 1954, Joan Weldon realized that giant, mutant ants were colonizing America and helped summon a military response. Sadly, James Whitmore lost his life fighting the ants.[4] And then, in 1956, Kevin McCarthy stumbled upon large pod-shaped organisms in transport across the United States. Once he realized they were aliens invading earth, he alerted medical authorities.[5] These are just a few examples. In the decades following Fermi's fateful lunch, hundreds of brave men and women have sounded alarms when they discerned external threats to humanity.

Why didn't anyone take these warnings seriously? After all, there is wreckage strewn across the entire planet, in the ocean, on the land mass, even traces are found in the sky, relics of a prolonged war against earth, enough evidence to fill hundreds of thousands of wagons, boats, cargo planes, boxcars, tractor-trailers, cargo ships, shipping containers, tankers, automobile trunks, suitcases, purses, and fifty-gallon drums. From the looks of it, earth is a battlefield and we *lost*.

This is where this book comes in. When archaeologists excavate a battlefield, they analyze the evidence, reconstruct the battle, and publish the story. This is what this book attempts to do - reconstruct the battle and tell the tale of the tactics, strategies, and outcomes of the conflict, all to alert the surviving generations.

The first chapter discusses the nature of the *relationship* between the intelligent life and this earth. The following four chapters present the *limits* to knowledge and understanding of the earth's natural systems. The third section, from chapters 6 to 12, discuss the flawed *approach* toward the earth's resources; the fabulous excess of connections, size, speed, quantity, range, noise, unsightliness, and greed. The fourth section, from chapter 13 to 24, assesses various *outcomes*, the current condition. The final chapter proposes *remedial action*, a new line of defense against the very thing that threatens the continued existence of the human race.

This is our moral inventory. We stagger up to the mirror and ask ourselves, "How did we end up in this mess?"

1. U.S. Department of Energy, Los Alamos National Laboratory, 'Where is everybody?" An account of Fermi's question, by Eric M. Jones, Report No: LA-10311-MS, 1981) doi:10.2172/5746675.

2. Robin Hanson. *The Great Filter — Are We Almost Past It?* 1998. Accessed October 14, 2019, http://mason.gmu.edu/~rhanson/greatfilter.html

3. *The Thing from Another World*. Directed by Christian Nyby. United States: Winchester Pictures Corporation, 1951.

4. *Them*. Directed by Gordon Douglas. United States: Warner Brothers, 1954.

5. *Invasion of The Body Snatchers*. Directed by Don Siegel. United States: Walter Wanger Productions. 1956.

Chapter 1: Global Rehabilitation

It is said that, in about five billion years, the Sun will enter the "red giant" phase, where it will expand in size, engulf our orbit and destroy all life on earth.

We couldn't wait.

On the morning of August 6, 1945, an apprentice electrician was dismantling his house, removing clay tiles from the roof, when he looked up and described "a gigantic fireball. It was at least five times bigger and 10 times brighter than the sun. It was hurtling directly towards me...It was the sound of the universe exploding."[1] His house was destroyed. He spent the next two months in a hospital recovering from his burns. When he returned to the ruins of his house, he found his father's pocket watch, blackened and rusty, the crystal blown away, with shadows of the hands fused into the dial, marking the time of the blast, 8:15 in the morning, the very moment the atom bomb exploded over Hiroshima.

With the radiance of ten suns burst forth at once in the sky, a new world was born at 8:15 am. Since then, over two thousand nuclear weapons have been tested in the atmosphere and underground. The largest, named Tsar Bomba, was 3,800 times more powerful than the one dropped on Hiroshima. The radiance of 38,000 suns. Even larger bombs have not been detonated because these lose most of their destructive

Looks like the sunset.
Atomic Test Able, Bikini Atoll.
Image: US National Archives.

energy to the atmosphere. Lost destructive energy, they say, is counterproductive. To give a sense of the destructive potential, the radius of total destruction of Tsar Bomba was 34 miles; third-degree burns were caused at 62 miles; a thermal pulse was felt at 170 miles; windows were broken at 560 miles. More windows were broken at greater distances by atmospheric focusing of the shock wave. To give a sense of the destruction, maps are created showing the blast rings superimposed over major cities.

Here is another sense. Many have taken the Great American Road Trip across the Dakotas and Wyoming, visiting the Badlands, Black Hills, Bighorn Mountains, Yellowstone, and beyond. A beautiful journey. Consider: If the blast were to occur over Deerfield Reservoir in the Black Hills, the entire hills ecosystem and community would be destroyed, third-degree burns would occur at Devil's Tower National Monument, a thermal pulse would be felt in the Cloud Peak Wilderness in the Bighorns and Fort Niobrara National Wildlife Refuge in Nebraska, and windows would be broken at St. Mary Visitor Center at Glacier National Park in Montana, Ripple Rock Nature Center at Capital Reef National Park in Utah, the Tallgrass Prairie National Preserve visitor center in Kansas, the St. Croix River National Scenic Riverway visitor center in Minnesota, the Park Theater Complex at Riding Mountain National Park in Manitoba, and the Grasslands National Park East Block Visitor Centre in Saskatchewan.

You are here.
58.6 megaton blast radius. Radius 1 = total destruction, 2 = third-degree burns,
3 = thermal pulse, 4 = broken windows.
Image: US Geological Survey

Stewardship

In recent years, there has been much talk about environmental stewardship. The concept has been clarified and enlarged since Aldo Leopold wrote these words in *A Sand County Almanac*: "There is as yet no ethic dealing with man's relation to land and to the animals and plants which grow upon it. The land-relation is still strictly economic, entailing privileges but not obligation."[2] Today, the concept of stewardship describes a mindset of responsible care for and intimate understanding of the biodiversity, sustainability, integration, and services of an ecosystem. Ultimately, the ecosystem is the earth.

Coincidentally, in recent years there has been much study of abusive relationships. Researchers have identified dozens of signs of an abusive partner. These include: 1) Speed: They move into a relationship too quickly, 2) Isolation: They separate the individual from their network of friends and family, 3) Dominance: They take control over the other person's life, 4) Exploitation: They force the other person to give up valuables, 5) Violence: They do physical harm. This can be difficult for some to recognize because of the false normalcy that can be established in long-term abusive relationships.

Speed. Thomas Jefferson predicted that it would take 1000 years to settle the land as far west as the Mississippi River.[3] Within 103 years of the Corps of Discovery expedition, the bison was nearly extinct, herds of cattle were being driven south to north and back, railroads crossed the territory, and homesteaders were staking claims. Land rush, gold rush, timber boom, oil boom, all were rapid expansions into territory with little, if any, consideration of long-term adverse impacts upon the ecology.

Isolation. Fencing, rails, roads, mines, farms, and cities fragmented the landscape, cutting off migration corridors and gene flow, progressively decreasing the size and quality of native habitat until, in the case of the tallgrass prairie, only 4% of the original remains, and that in small, widely scattered parcels threatened by invasives and loss of genetic diversity.

Dominance. The wild and native habitats were largely replaced by agricultural, urban, and industrial platforms, so that the native large mammals - bison, antelope, grizzly, elk, bighorn sheep, moose - were reduced to fractions of their original numbers and range. Old growth forests, prairies, wild rivers, wetlands, and many species within them saw a drastic reduction in numbers and extent. Leopold called it "man the conqueror...the land as slave and servant."[4]

Exploitation. As Leopold observed, the objective was economic gain via resource extraction. Oil, coal, gas, iron, gold, timber, soil, water and dozens of other commodities were removed from the land, usually leaving a degraded, damaged landscape behind. Many of these scars are visible today. Many sites are toxic.

Strip mine tailings, North Dakota. Image: US Geological Survey

Violence. A large percentage of the scientific community is developing "exciting" new ways to destroy humans and civilizations. The ultimate weapon, the doomsday machine, is already in service. An atomic blast properly placed, is so powerful that it vaporizes rock. It etches shadows in concrete. It can cause earthquakes. It sterilizes the ground. Turns sand into glass. This is not normal, rational behavior, it is violence against humanity and the earth.

Intervention

If these behaviors were conducted by an individual, it would be reasonable to conclude that the person was the perpetrator in an abusive relationship, perhaps irrational, delusional, even self-destructive. This is well understood. It has become commonplace as of late for public personas, upon being exposed as addicted, abusive, or violent, often all three occurring together, to enter a rehabilitation facility. Sometimes this comes after friends and family orchestrate a joint effort to convince the person that they have a serious problem requiring treatment. To benefit from the program, the individual needs to go beyond changing behavior, beyond simple abstinence - "white knuckling" - to changing the mind. The problem isn't the drinking, it's the thinking. The problem isn't in the hands, it's in the head.

Thus, some will benefit from treatment, remaking their thought processes, attitude, and behavior and, therefore, their relationships. And they live a well-adjusted life thereafter. But the road to recovery is a long one, requiring a lifetime of effort. In some treatment programs, a sponsor is needed. One addiction recovery program defines a sponsor as an addict "who has made some progress in the recovery program and shares that experience on a continuous, individual basis with another [addict] who is attempting to attain or maintain sobriety."[5]

We would do well to apply this to our relationship to the earth. A change is required in the individual and collective thought process, attitude, and behavior toward the earth. A moral inventory. An honest look in the mirror. And when we find ourselves backslidin', feeling that urge to overindulge in natural resources, to exploit the things around us without regard for consequence, to hoard the earth's riches, to blame others for our behavior, to manipulate the living and non-living things around us solely for our own personal benefit, and to resort to violence when we feel challenged, it is time to call for help. Don't try to fight yourself on your own.

As some in recovery are known to pray, "Give me courage to change the things which should be changed, and the wisdom to distinguish the one from the other."

Amen.

1. Vibeke Venema, "When time stood still. A Hiroshima survivor's story," *BBC News*, July 24, 2010, http://www.bbc.co.uk/news/special/2014/newsspec_8079/index.html

2. Aldo Leopold, *A Sand County Almanac and Sketches Here and There* (New York: Oxford, 1949), 203.

3. Albert Bushnell Hart, *Formation of the Union, 1750-1829* (New York: Longmans, 1892), 139.

4. Leopold, *A Sand County Almanac*, 260-1.

5. Alcoholics Anonymous, *Questions & Answers on Sponsorship* (New York: Alcoholics Anonymous World Services, Inc., 1983), 7.

Chapter 2: Bounded Rationality

It is fairly well known that the first World War brought the end of four great empires, the Ottoman, Austro-Hungarian, German, and Russian. In 1918, amidst the struggles for political power that ignited in the debris left by the fallen empires, sociologist Max Weber gave a lecture entitled *"Politics as a Vocation,"* which explored the legitimate basis for authority. He cited three: Tradition, Charisma, or Legal. Tradition being the "mores sanctified through the unimaginably ancient recognition and habitual orientation to conform." Charisma was the "absolutely personal devotion and personal confidence in revelation, heroism, or other qualities of individual leadership." Legal was "the belief in the validity of legal statute and functional 'competence' based on rationally created rules."[1]

Sadly, we do not find any reference to a fourth legitimate basis for authority: Knowledge, or its derivatives understanding and wisdom. Even if it were recognized, we are witnesses to an insurrection, coup de tat, revolution, a rebellion against informed authority. The marchers throwing increasingly larger rocks at each other carry posters that say, *"Down with Book Learnin."*

A few decades later it came to this: Some of the elderly still in circulation may recall talk of famine in China during the 1950's and 1960's. In many minds, China became synonymous with famine. During that time period, when a child would not finish his meal, parents and grandparents would say something like, "Eat your supper, there are people starving in China." The scraps would be thrown out to the birds.

There is a bird in black spruce bogs named White-throated Sparrow (*Zonotrichia albicollis*). Black spruce bogs are an acid peatland found in northern reaches of North America. They developed in ice block depressions of pitted outwash plains and moraines that were formed by continental glaciers during the Wisconsonian Ice Age. In addition to black spruce, they support tamarack, leatherleaf, cranberry, Labrador tea, and wire sedge. During the spring and early summer, it is possible to hear the plaintive call of the White-throated Sparrow in these bogs. Some say it sounds like, "*Old Sam Peabody, Peabody, Peabody.*"[2] Others say it sounds like, "*Sweet, sweet Canada, Canada, Canada.*"[3] It is the song of the northern bogs, capturing sunny days in a vast, spiced wilderness. But the bogs are getting quieter as of late, as we see the rise of the silent forest. Reports say that White-throated Sparrows number about 140 million in North America, but they are declining in numbers and range; it is reported that there has been a 63% decline in population and 35% decline in range since 1966. Primary causes are habitat loss, window collisions, and domestic cats.

Chairman Meow.

Birds have regional dialects and their songs change over time - in fact, many are adapting their songs to compete with urban noise pollution.[4] The White-throated Sparrow has regional dialects. Those from Quebec seem to be saying, "*Seize the bird property, property, property,*" those from Minnesota sound as if they are saying, "*Hey, what's with that saw, that house, that cat, out here?*" and those from Michigan sound like, "*You idiots, big idiots, idiots, idiots.*"

But 140 million sounds like a lot of sparrows. American Tree Sparrows (*Spizella arborea*) number about 20 million, Field Sparrows (*Spizella pusilla*) about seven million, Song Sparrows (*Melospiza melodia*) about 130 million, House Sparrows (*Passer domesticus*) about 540 million, Eurasian Tree Sparrow (*Passer montanus*) currently number about 50-100 million birds. There are perhaps a hundred species of Old World and American Sparrows. There may seem to be an endless supply. This could explain why in Palestine some 2000 years ago, two sparrows sold for less than five cents and five sparrows sold for less than 10 cents. Purchased in bulk, one would save 20%. A dime a dozen.

The Ecology of Scapegoats

During the 1940's, just prior to the Chinese famine, humans in China numbered in the hundreds of millions. There seemed to be an endless supply. At the same time, food production was struggling, and it wasn't meeting the needs of the Chinese populace. Someone saw Eurasian Tree Sparrows eating grain. Someone concluded that the sparrows were the cause of the shortfalls in food production. Chairman Mao was informed about it. Few dared to speak up and say that the shortage could be attributed to collectivization, grain procurement, or Lysenkoism.

So, having pinned crop failures on a two-cent bird, in 1958, Mao launched the *Four Pests* campaign, a nationwide effort to completely eradicate flies, mosquitoes, rats, and, yes, the Eurasian Tree Sparrow. "No warrior shall be withdrawn until the battle is won," declared the *Peking People's Daily*. "All must join battle ardently and courageously; we must persevere with the doggedness of revolutionaries."[5]

Over the course of about two years, hundreds of millions of Chinese citizens attacked the sparrows with slingshots, stones, and guns. Banging pots, pans, and drums and waving flags kept them aloft until they died of fatigue. Nests were raided, eggs were destroyed, and chicks were crushed. The public health campaign was a great success. By 1962, the people had killed one billion sparrows.

However, their heroic efforts to bring death upon on billion sparrows also brought death upon about 45 million Chinese, death by starvation. This campaign revealed exact exchange rate, about 22 sparrows per human, meaning one human would be worth a little over 40 cents if China were Palestine. The public health disaster was a great success. While Mao was told that sparrows ate grains, apparently, he did not know that Eurasian Tree Sparrows also ate locusts and were essential in their control. Thus, as the sparrow declined, locust populations increased, free to prowl the farmlands with impunity. As locust populations increased, crops were devastated, yields declined, food became scarce, famine swept the land, and 45 million humans starved to death. They might have been better off eating the sparrows.

"Eliminating the Last Sparrow." Part of the IISH / Stefan R. Landsberger / Private Collection; chineseposters.net

We Hurt Because It's What We Don't Know

Yes, the connectivity of nature, who would have known? Kill a wolf in Yellowstone, and aspen trees die. Bring zebra mussels into the Great Lakes and loons die of botulism. Kill the sparrows in China and people starve to death. Everything is connected to everything, a web of life. There are ecological niches to be filled and predator/prey relationships to maintain. It is a tightly choreographed ballet: remove one performer and others will stumble and fall flat.

As it is, humans, when armed with shovels and drums and lacking the knowledge and understanding of the inter-ecology of life and the outcomes of their actions, can become a natural disaster, a force that can reshape the planet. This is repeated on an ecosystem level every day. We have yet another list: kudzu, Bisphenol A, cats on Macquarie Island, rosy wolfsnail in Hawaii, possum shrimp in Flathead Lake, rabbits in New Zealand, ballast in the Great Lakes, fungus on spelunkers, Didymo algae on hip waders in New Zealand, brown snakes in airplane wheels, antibiotic-resistant microbes, *Caulerpa taxifolia* in the Mediterranean, fracturing wells in Oklahoma, desert irrigation, cities on floodplains, hydroelectric dams, plowing the shortgrass prairie. A long list of environmental actions with unforeseen and unintended bad consequences, naturally disastrous human behavior. This reveals something about our nature: We exhibit *bounded rationality*; our knowledge has limited scope. We don't have the breadth of vision.

On a Clear Day, I Can See Statistics

To combat this problem, humans conduct research, sweeping the literature and living sources for data, especially concerning the projected impacts of a proposed action upon the environment. In some quarters, these sweeps are called *Effects Analysis*. Ideally, we attempt to anticipate all possible negative impacts, effects, or outcomes of a given action upon species or their habitat. In reality, we try to see all likely and unacceptable possible outcomes. That shrinks the possibility pool considerably. But, inevitably, we miss something, like locust plagues.

To see all possible outcomes, good, bad, or indifferent, is impossible. But we come closer to this ideal as we assign more minds to the task, registering more possible outcomes - the effect of magnesium deficiency on soybeans, the effect of calcium deficiency on soybeans, the effect of nitrogen deficiency on soybeans. Go through all 118 of the elements on the periodic table, from Hydrogen to Ununoctium. Then go through all 80,000 edible plants. Then the rest of the plants. Then all mammals. Birds. Fish. Mollusks. Arthropods. Dinosaurs. Eventually, we run out of time, scientists, funding, imagination, and access.

Here is where Mathematicians save the day. We also approach this ideal through statistics, where we take a representative sample of the whole and make inferences about the whole. The greater and more random the sample, the more confidence there is in the conclusions about the whole. Through our finite data, we generate a statistical probability of something immeasurable: infinite reality. Sort of like finding the address of an electron. Or like gazing at the stars; we only perceive points of light, while those points, in actuality, are blinding spheres that dwarf our sun. We don't have the perspective, the breadth of vision, but we can use statistics to describe what is beyond our knowledge.

Unfortunately, Math doesn't always add up. There are various reasons for this, including sampling error, design flaws, response bias, and unmeasured factors. In fact, conclusions are given a margin of error. In negative findings, we can only say that it is unlikely that the project will have negative environmental impacts. There are degrees of unlikelihood; legal environmental documents use the terms, "discountable" or "insignificant". In the end, recognition of these inherent deficiencies brings us to the conclusion that we cannot disprove the existence of negative outcomes, only tell the probability of existence. We could call a very low probability a "Russell's Teapot", after Bertrand Russell, who discussed a teapot that may exist in space between the Earth and Mars but had not been disproved. His argument was that belief in something does not follow when it cannot be proven to be wrong.[6]

History is full of surprises.

So, in a more or less benign way, what plagued Mao plagues all of us. He was unaware, unable, or unwilling to see both the connections in nature and the future effects of his actions upon the environment. This is our nature.

Thus, having exhausted all efforts to attain complete knowledge of potential impacts, a negative finding is considered the final word, and the project proceeds apace. Gentlemen, start your bulldozers. At this point the project becomes an experiment, poking the earth to see how it reacts. We stand by and cringe. Somewhere in the forest, a sparrow falls to the ground and nobody hears it.

Wanted: An Infinite Number of Scientists

All of this would be irrelevant if, individually or collectively, we had the ability to consider all factors and possible outcomes. Ah, to have an infinite number of minds working on a 16,000-acre site where a nuclear weapons facility was proposed, each considering a different factor or outcome. Or better yet, for one person to have an infinite amount of time to think about the project, for this would enable us to gather all data and make statements of absolute certainty about the outcomes of the proposed project and, being an eternal study, the radioactive material would decay into simple lead and the project would be scrapped - and the marchers would put down their rocks, stop marching, and just stand there holding signs that say, "*World Peace by*

Doin Nothin." The business community cringes, "This is going to cost us." Maybe a better idea is to save the time and manpower and just find one infinite scientist.

A Finite History

Nah. Projecting from thousands of years of human ecological history, it can be said that the majority would reject an absolutely informed authority and that this conclusion has a margin of error of zero percent.

If knowledge is a legitimate basis of authority, and humans are bounded by a lack of critical or absolute knowledge, then humans have been overstepping their bounds. Outrunning their headlights. It works well for those exercising this authority to have social support by the growing crowd that rejects informed authority. We have been reduced to the other three justifications. It is our tradition to authorize charismatic figures and to write it into law.

1. Max Weber, *Essays in Sociology*, trans. H. H. Gerth and C. Wright Mills (New York: Oxford University Press, 1946), 79-80.

2. David Allen Sibley, *National Audubon Society, The Sibley Guide to Birds* (New York: Alfred A. Knopf, 2000).

3. Donald Stokes and Lillian Stokes, *Stokes Field Guide to Birds. Western Region* (New York: Little, Brown, and Company, 1996).

4. Irwin Nemeth and Henrik Brumm. "Birds and Anthropogenic Noise: Are Urban Songs Adaptive?" *Am Nat.* 176(4) (October 2010): 465-75

5. "Red China: Death to Sparrows," *Time Magazine*, May 5, 1959.

6. John G. Slater, *The Collected Papers of Bertrand Russell, Vol. 11: Last Philosophical Testament, 1943–68* (Abington: Routledge, 1983).

Chapter 3: Disinformation

In the hunt for endangered species, it is often said, "Absence of evidence is not evidence of absence." There is an alluring symmetry to that phrase, fitting nicely into the popular image of a universe that rests on elegant and concise laws. However, the order of our current reality may not match it without unsavory complexities.

Here is an elegantly simple equation: As goes the wilderness, so goes the wildlife.

A War That Roosevelt Lost

Prior to the Civil War, the southern old-growth swamp and forest extended from Texas to Illinois to North Carolina and Florida, and south to Cuba. This was the southern United States. After the Civil War, logging companies stripped the forest to such an extent that, by the 1930's, only a few relict stands of southern old-growth forest remained. This forest was the obligatory habitat of a bird named the Ivory-billed Woodpecker (*Campephilus principalis*), making it a specialist species, one that requires a narrow range of habitat, in contrast to one that can live in a wide variety of habitats, things like raccoons, starlings, goldfish, or sausage links. The bird is one of the largest woodpeckers on earth, spectacular, with a wingspan nearly three-feet wide, earning it the common name, *Good God Bird*.

As one might expect if one had informed expectations at that time, as the forest was stripped, the bird declined. By the 1920's, the species was rarely seen. Reasonably, ornithologists were alarmed. Some set out to survey and protect the species. In 1924, two ornithologists found a pair of nesting birds in Florida. They set up camp away from the nest. While away, two taxidermists armed with permits shot the birds. In

1932, a Louisiana politician, determined to prove the species was not in peril, got a hunting permit and shot one of the birds along the Tensas River, within an 80,000-acre remnant of southern old-growth forest named the Singer Tract, owned by the Singer Sewing Machine Company and managed by the Chicago Mill and Lumber Company (CMLC). This tract was one of the last strongholds of the bird.

Nobody home.

In 1938, logging began on the tract. At that time, ornithologist James Tanner was studying the Ivory-billed Woodpecker in the tract for his Ph.D. dissertation for Cornell University. In 1939, he estimated between 22 to 24 birds remained in existence and eight were in the Singer Tract. Alarmed at the logging, he developed a management plan that would retain some old growth stands and allow a mix of select and clear-cutting, with the hope that the plan would retain enough old growth to protect the species. The CMLC rejected his proposal. By 1941, most of the tract was being heavily logged. The president of the Audubon Society appealed to U.S. President Franklin Roosevelt. Roosevelt directed the Secretary of the Interior to save the land. The governors of Louisiana, Arkansas, Tennessee, and Mississippi backed the effort and wrote a letter to the CMLC. The Louisiana governor pledged $200,000 to save the property. The refuge director for the U.S. Fish and Wildlife Service and the Louisiana Conservation Commissioner met with the board chairman of CMLC and made a proposal.

The CMLC rejected the proposal.

The efforts to save the tract actually served to accelerate the logging. In 1944, another Audubon staff member saw an Ivory-billed Woodpecker in the tract by John's Bayou. He notified Audubon staffer and wildlife artist Don Eckelberry, who headed south to John's Bayou and followed the bird for two weeks. It was a female and had taken up roost in a tree. It was in a small patch of old growth surrounded by clear-cuts, watching as loggers took down the very trees it used for food. Eventually, the entire tract was logged, and that bird was never seen again. It is survived by Eckelberry's artwork which is in a museum in Wausau, Wisconsin. This was the last certified sighting of an Ivory-billed Woodpecker.

It is noteworthy that the offices of the Chicago Mill and Lumber Company at 129 North Washington Street in West Helena, Arkansas were preserved and honored on the National Register of Historic Places in 1996. The building was torn down in 2013. It is now a vacant lot where nobody is home. It is not clear if the ground was or was not sown with salt.

Apparently, logging set the birds free. Today, the Ivory-billed Woodpecker is a Category 6 bird, meaning it is "definitely or probably extinct". Probably, in that, numerous intriguing but controversial sightings of what may be Ivory-billed Woodpecker have occurred since 2004.[1]

Thus, the urgency of small populations. Minimum viable populations are a trap door, below which a species free-falls to its death. Extirpation is urgent, Endangerment is critical, Extinction is forever. This is what we have got.

That phrase, "Absence of evidence is not evidence of absence" is cited when one fails to find a rare species in a given project area, the intent being restraint. Restrain everyone from the conclusion that it has been proven that the rare species does not exist in the project area, and that, therefore, they are free to drill, blast, clearcut, excavate, dump, defoliate, and pillage. This phrase is implicit in the summary section of many environmental impact reports. This phrase needs a larger context.

The Birth of an Industry

Here it is: It is well documented that some 60 years ago, the tobacco companies, under the advice of their lawyers, began a campaign to render unrecognizable the notion that there was a connection between tobacco and cancer. Their strategy was to pay scientists to skew research and to cherry-pick research that showed no link. But beyond that, they produced a steady stream of public statements that there was "no clinical evidence," "no substantial evidence," "no laboratory proof," it was "unresolved" and "still open," not "statistically proven," "scientifically proven," or "scientifically established," and there was no "scientific causality," "conclusive proof," or "scientific proof."[2] The objective was to confuse the public by manufacturing doubt which created a false controversy which led consumers to conclude that they were free to smoke and chew with impunity. Ingenious. One can picture the executives sitting back and lighting up congratulatory cigars. Suggested Surgeon General's Warning: Cigar celebrations protect free speech.

This is strange. Biologists may not have considered that they were using the same terminology that the tobacco companies used to create confusion, to "keep the controversy open." On one hand, biologists use this argument to delay environmental degradation, and on the other hand, the tobacco companies used this argument to delay improved health. A two-edged sword. Although this was 60 years ago, they succeeded in befuddling the public, at least for a few moments, not about tobacco, but about the potency of absence. If something is not discovered, does that mean that it may exist? It is alleged, but we have ignored the proof, that there are television programs devoted to people who are searching for Bigfoot. Sasquatch. Yeti. How does one determine that something does not exist? Does it require absolute and infinite knowledge to make that statement? Apparently, some television producers want the public to believe so. Stay tuned for Episode Infinity: *We Are Gods*.

This is new. They argue, where there is a plethora of nothing, where there has been a consistent absence of empirical evidence of something, as negative results accumulate, possible existence always remains, and, here is the new idea, possible existence is powerful enough to balance or exceed any number of negative results. Thus, our world houses possible mermaids, unicorns, aliens, griffens, dragons, six-foot-eight tall invisible pucas, Russell's Teapot, fairies, Sasquatch, elves, zombies, werewolves, angels on the head of a pin, and healthful cigarettes. What was once impossible is now possible. What is this? We know of no sober biologists searching for pucas.

Disinformation Swarm

This may remind many of the movie *North by Northwest*, an old Alfred Hitchcock thriller whose violent climax occurs on the forehead of Thomas Jefferson. In this movie, there is a train station scene. The protagonist, Cary Grant, is being chased by the police. To evade them he pays a railroad baggage handler, called a "Red Cap", to give him his uniform. Grant changes into the uniform and walks right by the police. Shortly afterward, the police realize that he is dressed as a baggage handler, chase him into the train station, and lose him in a crowd of railroad baggage handlers, all wearing the same uniforms with the red cap.[3]

Each of those men in the red caps is a possibility, the real wanted man. The more men in red caps, the more possibilities, and the more trouble there is identifying the real wanted man in the red cap.

In the U.S., the subject of climate change is controversial, or it is claimed to be controversial by those that dispute it – currently, about one out of three US citizens doubt the planet is getting warmer or that humans have caused it. Meanwhile, there is a swarm of disinformation about the level, history, and origin of atmospheric carbon, the historic temperature of the earth, climate cycles, environmental profiteering, scientific fraud, consensus, dissent, and a hundred more topics. Each of these serves as a possible explanation for what is claimed to be a changing climate.

Men in red caps are everywhere. Now, it would be a restful thing if each possible explanation was weighted as to credibility, like horses at the racetrack. That mudder with the wooden leg, he has 25 to 1 odds. And the mare being wheeled off on a stretcher, don't even think about it, she is 50 to 1. But that's not the case here. Any possible explanation is being presented with weight equal to that of a carbon-fueled climate change. It is as if all the horses had 1 to 1 odds. This isn't fair, right, or real. Everyone except the oddsmaker is going to lose his shirt.

There is data. Data is about as close to objective reality that a subjective being can get. However, data is going the way of the wooden pencil. It is as if, when someone is told it is 75 degrees out, he retorts, "That's what *you* think!" So, maybe this the final product of the disinformation industry, when they assert that that objective reality is not objective reality, that the red cap is not a red cap. Dumbfounded in this new reality, there is suddenly no need to look for a man in a red cap.

Global Solipsism

It has been overheard, "We are living in a post-truth world."

This is the larger context for what is thought to be evidence-based perception. While many aged ones amongst us hail from the 20th century, a world where numbers created realities - checkbooks, baseball scores, election outcomes, food exports, miles per gallon, hat sizes, megatons of TNT - this is approaching obsolescence. The information that we sift through on a daily basis to formulate perception, opinion, or decisions has become deliberately and inadvertently contaminated, even overwhelmed with skewed, cherry-picked, manufactured, and false data. Not content to contaminate the

natural environment with purportedly harmless products, this content has infiltrated our information, what we know, our minds, with the same. At the same time, the rational weight of evidence has been altered so that what is even remotely possible, virtually impossible, is considered of equal value, of equal potency to that which is demonstrably real.

This could make it hard to balance that checkbook. This is why children can't look under their beds at night. This is why witches were burned. This is what we have. As the absence of evidence increases, as more Ivory-billed Woodpeckers, Great Auks, Passenger Pigeons, Laughing Owls, and Carolina Parakeets drop out of sight, there is accumulating evidence that we no longer know and we no longer care about the difference.

1. Tamasin Cave and Andy Rowell, *A Quiet Word: Lobbying, Crony Capitalism and Broken Politics in Britain* (New York: Random House, 2014), 199.

2. Michael D. Collins, "Putative audio recordings of the Ivory-billed Woodpecker (Campephilus principalis)," *J. Acoust. Soc. Am.* 129(3) (December 2010).

3. *North by Northwest*. Directed by Alfred Hitchcock. United States: Metro-Goldwyn-Mayer, 1959.

Chapter 4: Mismeasurement

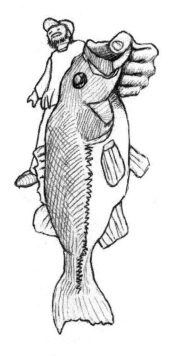

"Any action of an individual, and obviously the violent action constituting a crime, cannot occur without leaving a trace."[1] Those are the words of French criminologist, Dr. Edmund Locard, a pioneer in forensic science. Regarding a criminal, Paul Kirk stated it this way: "Wherever he steps, whatever he touches, whatever he leaves, even unconsciously, will serve as a silent witness against him."[2] Fingerprints, footprints, hair, fibers, scratches, broken glass, all of these are factual evidence, however trace they may be. A prized piece of evidence is the fingerprint. Like DNA, each human has a unique print, a unique pattern of arches, loops, and whorls. Get a good fingerprint at a crime scene and you have identified a criminal.

There are traces of human contact in the desert southwest. There, the Anasazi Indians marked their dwellings. Some marks were fingerprints impressed in the mud chinking, others were red and white handprints slapped on high rock walls. One mark that appears regularly across the barren, silent landscape is a single whorl, carved in stone or painted onto rocks.

National Park Service

Compared to What?

Today, there are green lawns in this desert landscape, apparently a sign of wealth and prosperity. But closer inspection reveals that the lawn is sprayed with a water-based green paint. Lawn dye. Grass paint.

Who would have thought? From all appearances, it is a lush, prosperous lawn. But step out of the context and compare it to an actual lawn, moist, photosynthesizing, and respiring, and any illusions of lushness are cast aside.

This leads to a realization: When we measure the condition of the landscape, it is valuable to compare the current wildlife condition, its population and range, to the wildlife condition that existed outside our current context, that of pre-settlement days, what is sometimes called Pre-Columbian North America. That is something that no longer exists. This means that it is valuable to measure what we see and what we *don't* see.

What we see: Looking across the vast agricultural landscape today, the wealth of mammal and bird stock may lead one to conclude that the current condition is a thriving animal community, vigorous, teeming, healthy. But, upon closer inspection, we find that the fauna is dominated by domestic and introduced animals. In the United States, for example, there are about 95 million cattle, 68 million pigs, five million sheep, nine billion chickens, 230 million turkeys, and, we might add, 120 million housecats and 90 million dogs. This list does not include the millions of Norway rats, city-dwelling mammals that appear to have assumed the role of a keystone species in the current commercial ecosystem and which are now quite able, through natural selection and the wonders of a sturdy western diet and untreated hormonal waste, to attain to the size of a healthy newborn humanoid. We assume that the breast meat accounts for most of this weight.

What we don't see: The majority of the original North American herds and flocks are, in comparative reality, extinct. Regarding the Pre-Columbian herds and flocks in North America, the archetypal example is the American bison. Numbering some 40 to 60 million animals, it once had a range of 4,500,000 square miles, from Mexico into northern Canada, the Great Basin Desert to the Appalachian Mountains. Today, 500,000 bison occupy about 55,000 square miles, about 1.2% of the original range, all of which is in preserves, ranches, and other confined space, and "in no place express the full range of ecological and social values of previous times."[3] The whorls of lines on the map below show the gradual collapse of the bison herd. At its nadir, only 541 bison remained. This was not natural selection at work.

Similar maps can be presented for hundreds of other mammals, birds, reptiles, amphibians, fish, plants, and habitats that have experienced an extreme reduction in population and range over the past 250 years.

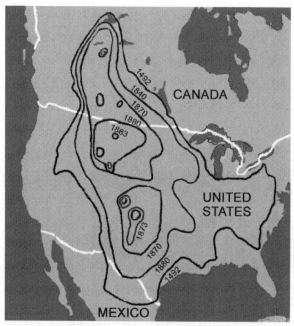

Fingerprint. Decline in Bison range.
Derived from: Library of Congress, Geography and Map Division. From William Hornaday's The Extermination of the American Bison, published in 1889.

There is a lesson in this: Just because a plant is green does not mean it is thriving. The same is true with natural ecosystems. Just because it is green or because it is teeming with animals does not mean it is thriving. The abundance of vegetation or animals alone does not indicate the actual condition of the landscape.

This becomes a pattern. As bison are a component of a herd, the herd is a component of an ecosystem. Thus, as falls the bison, so falls the prairie. Similar maps can be presented for many ecosystems that have experienced an extreme reduction in range over the past 250 years. Tallgrass prairie, prairie potholes, Great Lakes alvars, Oregon wet prairies, California vernal pools. It is difficult to project that the commercial ecosystems that have displaced the native ecosystems will escape the same retraction of range, given that they depend upon natural resources in one way or another. This concentric line pattern has become our collective fingerprint, the anthropogenic signature.

Meanwhile, research led by scientists at the University of Wyoming showed a 2% reduction in the size of trophy horns and antlers for 14 species of big game in North America. The study attributes this to hunting selection for trophy male animals.[4] While considering that fact, we are confronted with a complication: in certain parts of the United States, the illegal taking of wildlife now equals or exceeds the number of animals taken legally.[5] This is not natural selection at work.

So, this proves to be a volatile mixture. The ability to degrade our environment coupled with the willingness to violently break laws governing our environment, both man-made and natural, results in a precipitous decline of individuals, groups, and systems. That is to say, as a species, we have left our fingerprint: A series of concentric rings around an empty space.

1. Edmond Locard, *La police et les méthodes scientifiques*, (Paris, Éditions Rieder, 1934), 8

2. Paul Kirk, *Crime Investigation. Physical Evidence and the Police Laboratory* (New York: Interscience Publishers, Inc., 1953).

3. Kevin L. Monteith, Ryan A. Long, Vernon C. Bleich, James R. Heffelfinger, Paul R. Krausman, and R. Terry Bowyer, "Effects of harvest, culture, and climate on trends in size of horn-like structures in trophy ungulates," *Wildlife Monographs,* 183(1) (2013). doi:10.1002/wmon.1007

4. Ruth S. Musgrave, Sara Parker, and Miriam Wolok. "The Status of Poaching in the United States - Are We Protecting Our Wildlife?" *Natural Resources Journal*, 33(4) (1993).

5. Eric W. Sanderson, Redford, Kent H., Weber, Bill, Aune, Keith, Baldes, Dick, Berger, Joel, Carter, Dave, Curtin, Charles, Derr, James, Dobrott, Steve, Fearn, Eva, Fleener, Craig, Forrest, Steve, Gerlach, Craig, Gates, C. Cormack, Gross, John E., Gogan, Peter, Grassel, Shaun, Hilty, Jody A., and Jensen, Marv, "The Ecological Future of the North American Bison: Conceiving Long-Term, Large-Scale Conservation of Wildlife," *Conservation Biology*, 22(2)(2008): 252-266.

Chapter 5: Scientific Error

In the quest for scientific truth, there is little mention of the fact that, during the course of controlled experiment or the gathering of data, the failure of the soda pop machine to dispense the right change to the research scientists altered the outcome of the research to a statistically significant degree. That explains why the space capsule landed in another hemisphere, upside down. Not only did the soda pop machine have such an effect, but so did the bologna and mayonnaise sandwich that had been sitting on the windowsill in the sun all morning. And the brittle cataracts in the researcher's eyes. And the phone call in the afternoon from the cousin in jail asking for bail money. This is the Wonderful World of Science. Ignore the convict behind the curtain, you are looking at Scientific Fact.

A biologist may find himself thinking a lot about that phone call from the incarcerated relative, begging for lunch money and a pie with metal-file filling, as he walks about the forests, plains, and mountains in search of things, things that in all probability do not exist but cannot be excluded without an all-knowing frame of reference, which frame of reference can be approximated through statistically significant sample sizes, generally numbering well less than infinity, which, doggonit, invariably fail to consider that one sample that contains that which you, in the end, had assumed not to exist. Maybe if we maintain the sample size but enlarge the number of identical studies, we can exclude the possibility. Or maybe if we have a massive amount of people say the same thing, we can make it come true. Why, the sheer force of one's personality might do it, but we find ourselves straying from our mission which has been misplaced in the merger with our competition and the research staff lost track of things when they were furloughed for a month.

Random Variables

The boreal forest is one of the world's largest biomes, covering almost 12% of the earth's surface. It is characterized by long, cold winters, cool summers, thin soils, conifers, low precipitation, and, something omitted in most common descriptions, terrifying hordes of biting insects. Ticks, horse flies, deer flies, mosquitoes, no-see-ums, and the black fly. This is the place where camping vacations are laid to rest. A lazy day in June spent hiking about the boreal forest in search of something or other is a grand opportunity to observe these firsthand. You are, in fact, 1) A carbohydrate burning organism, 2) You exhale carbon dioxide, and 3) You attract carbon dioxide seeking organisms. Herein lies the Black Fly. The female black fly is sensitive to increased carbon dioxide in the air and it will seek out the origin in search of a blood meal. They do not bite or pierce like other insects, they saw you open with their tongue.

One can construct a rough gauge of one's "Carbon Footprint" by measuring exactly how many of such organisms are attracted to your organism. Determine the total surface area you occupy at any given moment and divide that into the total number of black flies that are stationed on you at that same moment. An average adult male has about 1.9 square meters of surface area, equal to the surface area of four ten-pound housecats or the surface area of the 40 bottles of Fonseca Vintage Port 1970 in the wine rack in the closet in the back of the lab The wine may be worse than the bologna and mayonnaise sandwich because many researchers would be unable to resist conducting a rigorous weekend regression analysis on the relationship between the bottles and something or other. Predictably, and this is with a high degree of confidence, they would carry out five repeated measurements involving eight independent variables over the course of two days. They would find that, after each measurement, the dependent variable approached zero. In their increased social confidence, they assert that *they are on to something.* The unknown parameter appears to be within reach. A loud argument breaks out as to the significance of the pizza delivery boy appearing seven times, clearly a random variable, but the exact function isn't known. Invariably, they abandon the study after the last measurement. All the while they had been carrying on, their personal mass and surface area had expanded beyond average, well beyond what anyone would have predicted, ruining the experiment design. The conversation between researchers degrades into insults and sobbing, a viewing of *The Spy Who Came in From the Cold*, followed by a deep slumber. Monday morning the phone rings as loud as church bells and it's someone's cousin again. So goes the Scientific Method.

Anyhow, one census of a black fly population that fed on an average adult male conducting a survey for endangered plant species in the boreal forest tallied 6,432 flies. This is some 3000 flies per square meter. Now to be useful, we need to measure the carbon output and we need to compare this to other carbon producers. But we have already determined that these are 6,432 random variables at any given moment in an environment where this man, of two square meters, is in search of a list of 100 rare species that depend upon his observation for their survival. Unfortunately, a century of resource extraction has created a third-growth recovering forest, stripped of old growth characteristics, choked with aspen clones, hazelnut thickets, mountain maple, and balsam fir budwormed deadfall, all being observed through the matrix of mosquito netting and the haze of fogged prescription glasses beaded with rain and perspiration, while an electrolyte-depleted circulatory system produces leg cramps and heat exhaustion, iron streaked rocks send the compass spinning like a roulette wheel, and the black flies sound like water torture as they pelt the insect proof clothing and this is supposed to determine the nonexistence of an object as large as a silver dollar in a 50-acre patch of forest.

The formula should read something like:

$$y_i = \beta_0 + \beta_1 x_{1i} + \cdots + \beta_p x_{pi} + \varepsilon_1 + \cdots + \varepsilon_{pi}$$

Where Y is the rare plant frequency and X represents independent variables including survey intensity, stand potential, phenological stage, light intensity, deadfall proliferation, drought index, spruce budworm kill factor, seral stage, deer density, slope, soil moisture, wind speed, surveyor education, surveyor experience, surveyor organizational skill, surveyor lactate levels, electrolyte imbalance, neurotransmitter depletion, excess body temperature, eyeglass opacity, cornea deterioration, cognitive disassembly, caffeine-induced confidence, memory loss, methamphetamine lab density, mosquito netting shear strength, boot porosity, pencil loss, blister quotient, degree of disorientation, fungal growth rate, bone fracture, anxiety level, battery failure, life insurance dollar amount, declining profit margins, and bitter regret. Each E represents one of 6,432 black flies.

We may be on to something. Here we begin to figure out the value of B. The dependent variable Y is inversely proportional to the value of the independent variable X and the error factor E. As X and E increase, Y decreases. So, let us get this straight: This is to say, as the probability of the existence of a rare species approaches zero, so do we.

Chapter 6: Disintegration

Many leaders in the entertainment, sports, religious, or political industries claim millions of devotees. Followers, fans, groupies, sycophants.

This is nothing new. After the Great War, Benito Mussolini, the leader of Italy, portrayed himself as the ideal male, the embodiment of hegemonic masculinity, virile, with supreme military, athletic, and musical abilities. Millions bought into this myth and became fans, including statesmen, writers, and religious leaders. Although his portrait still hangs in some households, his body was last seen hanging upside down outside a gasoline station in Milan.

It would be difficult to maintain one million friendships, anyhow. There is a limit to human cognition, memory, and time, all of which limit human ability to maintain stable relationships. Anthropologist Robin Dunbar suggested that the limit is about 150 relationships.[1] Some have cited the similar size of prehistoric communities, modern-day communes, business structures, and other social groupings as evidence supporting this number. This indicates that only visitors from other worlds could rightly claim one million friendships and that any making this claim should be held for observation immediately. This also indicates that when one acquires a new stable friendship, one has to be cast off, tossed into a pile, like those high school yearbooks in the attic. Knowing this can give one great pleasure at those moments when one has been expelled from a social circle; it is the happy news that your former friend just got a new friend! Hold those congratulations, however, they will not be able to comprehend it.

Yet, wildlife will group in the millions. Herds, flocks, schools. We return to the story of the American bison. In 1839, Thomas Farnham described a bison herd he encountered along the Santa Fe Trail in western Kansas, about 160 miles east of Bent's Trading Post:

> The buffalo during the last three days had covered the whole country so completely, that it appeared oftentimes extremely dangerous even for the immense cavalcade of the Santa Fe traders to attempt to break its way through them. We travelled at the rate of fifteen miles a day. The length of sight on either side of the trail, 15 miles; on both sides, 30 miles: - 15x3=45x30=1,350 square miles of country so thickly covered with these noble animals, that when viewed from a height, it scarcely afforded a sight of a square league [4,428 acres] of its surface.[2]

That herd was larger than Rhode Island. Now, if we compare that to the herd seen by Nathaniel Langford in 1862 near the Red River in North Dakota, we may get an idea of how many bison were in the Santa Fe Trail herd. Langford estimated the herd he saw covered 60 square miles and numbered one million bison.[3] The Santa Fe Trail herd was 23 times that size. If Langford's estimates were accurate and scalable, then the Santa Fe Trail herd may have numbered in the tens of millions.

However, these are not meaningful relationships; it is well beyond bison cognition to befriend 23 million bison. One study suggests that the primary function of groups is group and ecosystem stability: "Social groups rather than individuals are the basic building blocks around which predator-prey interactions should be modelled and that group formation may provide the underlying stability of many ecosystems."[4] Animal groupings, both predator and prey, serve for long-term stabilization of populations and ecosystems. They may also serve for mating opportunities and raising young.

Home range of animals has been defined as the area an individual occupies on a regular basis, but a more recent study defined it as "that part of an animal's cognitive map of its environment that it chooses to keep updated."[5] Cognition again. This physical range is matched by the bounds of its cognition.

Unfortunately, it appears that humans don't follow these rules. We have a mismatch between cognition and range and group size. We have a regrettable history of large group behavior. Our groups have quickly devolved into labor riots, ethnic purges, soccer melees, partisan rallies, traffic jams, rock concerts for geriatric rock musicians, and world wars. Riot police inevitably follow. Thus, it is possible to infer a human group of unsustainable and unmanageable size from the smell of tear gas. Some may reason that tear gas defines the edge of the natural human home range.

Thanks to each and every one of you for coming. You and you and you and...

Thus, if our social limit is less than 200 individuals, then the exaggerated grouping function seen in humans must be other than social. Studies claim that an initial cause of large grouping in humans was food security. The change from a subsistence, hunter-gatherer existence to an agricultural collective resulted in a dramatic improvement in food storage capacity and harvest stability. Security.

Today, the excessive grouping may be partly due to crowding. Just commuting to work one is in an overextended group. Couple that with expanded home range and the problem multiplies. Imagine if you had

37

the task of fitting as many third graders into a school bus as you could. It would be far easier to do this if they were all sedated rather than hepped up on corn syrup solids and red dye number 11. A bouncing atom takes more space than a motionless atom. This is why air bubbles rise in water, heat rises, thunderstorms build, insulation is deeper in attics than beneath floors, and angry people shout from balconies instead of cellars. So too with larger humans. When alive, we are like a sleeping bag released from a stuff sack; we require many times the space as a non-living human. Unfortunately, the task today is fitting 7.73 billion humans into a shrinking planet, a species hepped up on 9.5 million tons of coffee per year, corn syrup solids, coal tar blue, and artificial taste. On average, our space requirements exceed that from decades ago. Data from the US Census Bureau shows that since 1960, the average area of American housing has increased 50% while the household size has decreased by 24%.[6,7] Make that 7.74 billion.

In any event, the material and psychic damages of congestion in the urban zone are well documented. Ian Kuijt estimates that populations in the earliest settlements in Neolithic sites in the Near East had a mean of less than one hundred. As the centuries passed, the population numbers increased to the thousands. As the numbers increased, so did the complexity of the buildings, with the development of segmentation and multiple stories. After 2000 years, these villages were abandoned. Cause of abandonment may have been deteriorating sanitation, loss of privacy, interpersonal tensions, reduced ability to process information, reduced mobility, loss of economic homeostasis, social segmentation and differentiation, hierarchical social divisions, divisions of labor, and restricted diet.[8]

Kuijt summarizes it this way: "Under conditions of population aggregation, animals and humans respond negatively to a number of features in their environment: congestion, loss of control, loss of privacy and information load."[9] In other words, the exaggerated structure of civilized society caused the demise of civilized society.

They disintegrated. Perhaps they all split up into groups of 150 and went their separate ways.

Wish they would have said something. We passed 150 long ago. One million followers? Technology may make it possible for everyone to have 7.74, no, 7.75 billion followers. There isn't much open ground in that herd, and it would take about 240 years to pass this spot. Put up another story, build another cubicle. As humans devolve into larger groups, integrating everything, expanding beyond our cognitive abilities, a less ordered, less fit society results. The smell of tear gas is in the air.

1. R. I. M. Dunbar. (1992). "Neocortex size as a constraint on group size in primates". *Journal of Human Evolution*. 22 (6): 469–493.

2. Thomas J. Farnham, *Travels in the Great Western Prairies, the Anahuac and Rocky Mountains, and in the Oregon Territory* (Poughkeepsie NY: Killey & Lossing, 1841), 177.

3. Nathaniel P. Langford, *Vigilante Days and Ways* (Boston: J. G. Cupples Co., 1890).

4. John M. Fryxell, Anna Mosser, Anthony R. E. Sinclair, and Craig Packer, "Group formation stabilizes predator–prey dynamics," *Nature*, 449 (2007).

5. Powell, Roger A. and Michael S. Mitchell, "What is a home range?" *Journal of Mammalogy*, 93(4) (2012): 948–958.

6. U.S. Department of Commerce, *2017 Characteristics of New Housing* (2018), https://www.census.gov/construction/chars/

7. U.S. Census Bureau, *Current Population Survey, Annual Social and Economic Supplements, 1940 and 1947 to 2018* (2018), https://www.census.gov/programs-surveys/saipe/guidance/model-input-data/cpsasec.html

8. Ian Kuijt, "People and Space in Early Agricultural Villages: Exploring Daily Lives, Community Size, and Architecture in the Late Pre-Pottery Neolithic," *Journal of Anthropological Archaeology* 19(1) (2000): 75–102.

9. Kuijt, "People and Space," 78.

Chapter 7: Human Scale

John G. Williams Preserve in North Dakota is a Nature Conservancy property. It is famous for Piping Plover, a very rare, imperiled bird. In the spring, one might see a plover in the surf of Pelican Lake, an inland saline lake. This would be one of some 12-13,000 Piping Plovers in existence. Although this is a 70% increase since its all-time-low a few decades ago, it is still below its pre-settlement population. Working with numbers from the Great Lakes pre-settlement population, the pre-Columbian numbers may have been around 160,000 breeding pairs or a total population of 260,000 birds. That means our current population is about 5% of the original, up from 2%.

123-billion-acre Assisted Living Facility

This modest rebound in numbers give some sense of relief, since they put the species at what is believed to be sustainable population levels or above *minimum viable population*, where they find sufficient genetic variation, breeding opportunities, and breeding success to maintain population levels.

Regarding the recent success of Piping Plover in New Jersey, it was stated, "We need to continue our intensive management for a number of years to sustain any recovery."[1] A familiar outcome. This has become the predicament for most, if not all of the thousands of imperiled species on earth: they have become dependent upon human intervention for survival. Just a few hundred years ago, almost all of these species existed as self-sustaining populations that ultimately supported the ecosystem upon which *we* depended. We have witnessed a role reversal, from caretaker to caregiver.

Intensive management. History tells us that land management was the scheme that initiated habitat and species loss in the first place, our current "extinction crisis."[2] Clear cut forests to build ships and cities, mine iron to support war efforts, dam rivers to provide electricity and irrigation, plow prairies to provide grain for livestock and fuel for humans. In those land management systems that humans devised, native habitat was altered or destroyed, wildlife was targeted, and native populations declined to our present species-depleted world that now demands intensive management. The scheme has become Management Begets Management. How much land management would there be today if there had been no land management in the past? True, in our current reality, explosive population, resource demand, transoceanic transport, climate change, war, and other matters have forced us to look at that herd, coal seam, grassland, and wonder how we can exploit it. Whatever the reason, we have been brought to a resource management scheme that is comparable to hiring one person simply to dig a hole and another person simply to fill it in. If the hole wasn't dug in the first place, both workers could spend some time with their families admiring the non-excavated, virgin landscape at the *No Hole National Park*. It's like an arsonist fireman setting fire to homes, or insulin companies handing out free liters of soda pop, orthopedic surgeons wandering the streets at night breaking pedestrian legs with baseball bats, or masked policemen on a crime wave in a big city. Currently, it is a cycle, but whether it is an endless cycle, well, that depends.

There are hundreds of thousands of scientists in the world, many of which specialize in one aspect or another of land management: ecologists, hydrologists, wetland scientists, geologists, seismologists, range conservationists, interpretive rangers, geographers, cartographers, climatologists, ornithologists, zoologists, botanists, wildlife refuge managers, oceanographers, and so forth. If this were the year 1363, and the landscape was that prior to industrialization, colonization, and the invention of the first gun, we wonder what their work would entail.

As humans double down their intensive management, to the point of inventorying and labeling every individual tree in a forest, it can be a bettor's sport to watch these management schemes to see if humans have advanced so far as to ensure that their efforts to restore wildlife and habitat are enlightened enough that they do not repeat mistakes of the past or create new mistakes, which, in turn, require new schemes and we keep the science community occupied in something other than admiring that un-excavated, virgin prairie into the indefinite future, or at least until the species run out. After that, each of these scientists becomes, as Dr. Nick Lunn of the Canadian Wildlife Service is known to say, "a historian."[3]

Non-linear Retrogression

There are many graphs out there showing the change in wildlife populations since the industrial age, about the time that large-scale earth-moving projects came into being - Panama Canal, Welland Canal,

43

Fontana Dam. One controversial study stated that we have seen a loss of 52% of wildlife on earth in the past 40 years.[3] Another study showed we have seen a 29% decline in birds in North America since 1970.[4] Regardless of the controversy, similar statements are being made in studies of individual species or groups of species. A grand die-off in the near future, lines plunging downward. Fisheries will be depleted in 40 years, polar bears will be extinct in a few decades, neotropical birds, elephants, lions, rhinos, and so forth. Extrapolating current trends, there is a point on the line at which *there is no line.*

Extrapolation goes both ways. In one direction, we would get to the end of the curve naturally, assuming that we live indefinitely, which has been working out fairly well for those currently living. But how to get to the other end of the curve? How might we get to traveling back to 1804, when Lewis and Clark were floating up the Missouri River through a wildlife preserve ten times the size of the Serengeti, or 1673, when Jolliet was mapping out the Mississippi River, or 1541, when Coronado was on the Staked Plain of Texas and saw bison in such force that he said, "It is impossible to number them, for while I was journeying through these plains...there was not a day that I lost sight of them"[5]? Land management back then was a Native American setting a prairie fire. In three weeks, the green grass attracted bison and the bison attracted hunters and the hunters attracted camp cooks, a sort of trophic cascade.

Some Things Never Change

Habitat determines niche. Niche has a certain predictability. Species will require a fairly consistent set of parameters in order to persist and thrive. Thus, biologists have defined habitat requirements for many species. A geographic database query can identify the intersection of habitat characteristics that meet the habitat requirements of the species. This point in ecospace has a higher probability of supporting a population of the species. Armed with this geodata, a surveyor can locate that intersection on the actual landscape with the hopes of finding a population of a species persisting and thriving. He also avoids wasting time and energy on landscapes with low probabilities, such as a golf course or pet cemetery. This "predictive habitat distribution modeling" works well in the field.

44

We can attribute this degree of predictive success to the relatively static niche requirements of a species. We say species because, at the genus level, the amount of variance in habitat requirements between similar species of the same genus can be great. Think snow leopard versus jaguar. Within a species, even across its range, there is a recognizable level of homogeneity. Consider the Piping Plover (*Charadrius melodus*). The three populations (Atlantic Coast, Northern Great Plains, and Great Lakes) all have very similar habitat requirements: "wide, flat, open, sandy beaches with very little grass or other vegetation."[6]

Just Who Do We Think We Are

Relatively static niche requirements are so because the nature of most species is relatively static in the human time frame. Extinct bison (*Bison priscus*) were found in the Mammoth Steppe, a habitat similar to the prairie habitat that modern bison (*Bison bison*) occupy. However, social media algorithms notwithstanding, it has become hard to say this about humans. There were many centuries where humans exhibited consistent habitat requirements. The real estate ads from any century prior to the Industrial Age read:

```
HOUSE FOR SALE - Affordable single-room, wooden home
with bark, leather, or grass roofing and outdoor plumb-
ing. In quaint village with community garden and water-
front access in temperate to tropical climate. Ask about
our easy credit terms. Call Mr. C. Magon HI. 5-4056
```

Something like that. But this is not the case today. Looking at the human species across its range, for all races, ethnic groups, and nationalities, our habitat and niche breadth has expanded. As one report said, "Humans are remarkable for their ability to adapt to new niches much faster than the time required for genetic change."[7] Indeed. We have what is called "adaptive phenotypic plasticity."

What would predictive habitat distribution modeling show for humans? The point would be lost because we occupy everywhere. Adaptively, we find us in everything from urban high-rise settings to galvanized steel huts in landfills outside Mexico City, lonely caves in Afghanistan, bombed out cinderblock rubble in Syria, a North Face

VE25 at 26,000 feet, even tiny houses orbiting 254 miles above the earth. But do we change entirely out of adaptive strategy?

The beaver invades a lowland filled with eastern red cedar, builds a dam, and the lowland fills with water and the cedar dies. The beaver

didn't adapt to the wetland, it created the wetland. Fortunately, beavers do not have the ability to run a forest harvester. Unfortunately, we do. We also can run dragline excavators, row crop tractors, river dredges, and tower cranes. The ecological niche that humans occupy is fluid, plastic, shifting. We occupy villages at 16,732 feet in the Andes to 918 feet below sea level in the Jordan Valley, permafrost to salt flats, sand deserts to rainforests, underground tunnels to treetops, vegetarian to carnivore, monogamous to polygamous. So much of this is not an adaptive response, but because we have unique, advanced cognitive and behavioral mechanisms, the ability to change our nature. We don't wait for mutations to occur, we self-mutate.

As a result, our habitat requirements are not static. Armed with machinery, we alter the world around us to suit our current fancies, building a great variety of uniquely human habitats. Impoundments, farm belts, Levittown's, Soviet Apartments, artificial islands, gated communities, mansions, man camps, trailer parks, communes, nomadic camps, floating villages, and, finally, the back of a Dodge van.

This might remind everyone of the tragic figure, Lt. Colonel Glenn Manning.[8] It was 1957. One day, Glenn was a simple army officer engaged to marry his sweetheart, Carol Forrest, and a few days later he was 50-feet tall, wearing mutant-sized diapers, tossing automobiles with his left hand, and smashing the Las Vegas Sands Hotel with his right. At the last, he was headed to drink up Lake Mead, but he never made it that far. He grew way too big. And he had gone mad.

Well, we too have grown way too big. But this is not an adaptation, it is not genetic change brought about by an atomic plutonium bomb exploding at a bomb tower surrounded by Hollywood actors at a military site at Desert Rock, Nevada. No, our unique cognitive and behavioral mechanisms enable us to change our nature. "Free Will", if you will. This decision to change has moved us to depart from our historic ecospace and it demands a changed set of habitat conditions.

In our current phenotype, we have greatly widened our niche breadth, increased our consumption, expanded our diet, expanded our range, overlapped other niches, and, as a result, have found ourselves in conflict and competition with a host of species historically outside of our boundaries.

Horribly, within a year, Lt. Colonel Manning was followed by Nancy Archer,[9] "a wealthy but highly troubled woman with a history of emotional instability and immoderate drinking."[10] She too, grew to 50 feet in height and attacked everything in her path, including her two-timing, no-good husband, Harry, and his gold-digging girlfriend. Overconsumption is not gender biased.

Back to Nature

The scale of our projects, developments, structures, and systems has exceeded our niche. We are occupying so much ecological space that we have become predator, prey, parasite, mutualist, subterranean, aquatic, aerial, terrestrial, all at once. Hydra, we of many heads. Soon, there will be little room for anyone else, except, perhaps, those army men with bazookas trying to bomb us back to 1363. Good luck, boys. We have outreached the human scale and are now operating at an outsized scale beyond *Tyrannosaurus rex*, more akin to that occupied by Godzilla or the reckless gods of old; Hecatoncheires, Cormoran, Fachen, Hiranyaksha, Quinametzin, Ojáncanu.

Those were myths. We are real, but of mythic proportions, a race of 50-foot-tall, colossal humans, eating cars, throwing palm trees, oversized and overfed and still growing. Various studies state that if all people on earth lived like the average North American, it would take about four earths to sustain us. We have a fight on our hands but put away those weapons. The battle begins with 'our unique behavioral and cognitive mechanisms', to know how to fit and to choose to fit. With all the talk of sustainable resource use, without downsizing, reducing what we do to eye-level, village-sized, below-the-treetops, human scale, this colossus is unsustainable; it is on the verge of drinking the entire earth dry.

1. Todd Pover and Christina Davis, "Piping Plover Nesting Results in New Jersey: 2015." Conserve Wildlife Foundation of New Jersey. Retrieved from http://www.conservewildlifenj.org/downloads/cwnj_658.pdf

2. Bruce A. Wilcox and Dennis D. Murphy, "Conservation Strategy: The Effects of Fragmentation on Extinction," *The American Naturalist*, Vol. 125(6) (June 1985), 879-887

3. Tom Schueneman, "Scientist on Western Hudson Bay Polar Bear Population: 'I Consider Myself a Historian.'" PlanetWatch, March 10, 2008,

https://earthmaven.io/planetwatch/biodiversity/scientist-on-western-hudson-bay-polar-bear-population-i-consider-myself-a-historian-eG-fssfST0eig-54SdvAPg/

4. WWF. "Living Planet Report 2016. Risk and resilience in a new era." Gland, Switzerland: WWF International, 2016, http://awsassets.panda.org/downloads/lpr_2016_full_report_low_res.pdf

5. George P. Winship, *Coronado's journey to New Mexico and the great plains* (New York: A. Lovell, 1894), 580.

6. U.S. Fish and Wildlife Service, *Endangered Species Facts. Piping Plover* [Fact sheet] (2001).

7. Daniel Nettle, Mhairi A. Gibson, David W. Lawson, and Rebecca Sear, "Human behavioral ecology: current research and future prospects." *Behavioral Ecology*, Volume 24(1) (September 2013): 1031–1040

8. *The Amazing Colossal Man.* Directed by Bert I. Gordon. United States: American International Pictures, 1957.

9. *The Attack of the 50 Foot Woman.* Directed by Nathan Juran. United States: Woolner Brothers Pictures Inc., 1958.

10. *Wikipedia, The Free Encyclopedia,* s.v. "The Attack of the 50 Foot Woman," (Accessed April 15, 2019), https://en.wikipedia.org/wiki/Attack_of_the_50_Foot_Woman

Chapter 8: Uniformitarianism

Until recently, humans had been taking a leisurely stroll through a comparatively placid geological epoch known as the *Holocene*, the latter part of the Quaternary period, which epoch began at the end of the last glaciation. This is no longer the case. As far back as the 1930's a discussion began that we have entered another epoch that is characterized by the dramatic reshaping of earth's geology, chemistry, and ecology by human beings, particularly since the advent of atomic weapons in 1945 and certainly since the years marked by anthropogenic climate change. In the early 1980's, it was suggested that this new epoch should be named the *Anthropocene*. Anthropos, as in humans. It has also been suggested that this epoch should be named the *Eremocene*, with reference to the mass depletion of species and populations on the earth due to human activity. Eremite, Latin for recluse. Some suggested that it be renamed the *Homogecene*. That is, homogeneus, Latin for similar race, family, or kind, a nod to the growing uniformity of ecosystems and species around the world. Others have suggested it be named the *Plasticene*, with reference to the thick layer of useful and convenient plastic that has accumulated on the earth's surface, much like shrink wrap around a ball of decaying ground beef. Plastic, as in plastic. It might be suggested that it may be named the *Frankencene*, with reference to the genetically modified monstrosities that may someday terrorize quaint villages around the earth. Franken, not as in sense.

What are these things, anyhow? Looking at the eight-foot-tall, rubber-skinned, man-shape with electrodes on the neck raises serious doubts about its humanity and it is this fuzzy ethic that freed its creator

to pursue the creature to its death on an ice floe in the Arctic some 200 years ago. This has become the norm in our Space Age. Consider: Michael Graham took an axe to the horribly fused reintegration of two laboratory assistants named "Samuels" and "Dale" in 1965.[1] He was never charged. So too with Herbert Marshall, who, in 1958, ignored David Hedison's plaintive cries for help and crushed the poor man with a rock when he was at his most vulnerable half-fly, half-man

If he were alive today

incarnation.[2] Marshall spent the remaining eight years of his life a free man and was rewarded with a star on the Hollywood Walk of Fame. The horror.

Why are these things, anyhow? The common allegation is that natural selection rewards favorable traits acquired and expressed in an individual species, selecting that individual for survival, moving that species toward a fitter condition, a higher state. In any event, armed with that creed, attempts have been made to speed up this process

through various schemes. This has brought humankind mutation induction, eugenics, and gene splicing. Mutation induction was applied to humans during atomic blasts and nuclear power plant meltdowns in the past century and no favorable traits could be recovered from the sparkly radioactive ash. Eugenics, touted by major politicians in the past century from the eastern and western hemispheres, threatened to turn mankind into a mammalian version of the Irish potato. Gene splicing brought the promise of strawberry flavored fish or fish flavored strawberries, but as applied to humans, would instead bring us a race of eight-

Sergeant Frank

foot-tall military police. Better living through genetics. But that's not what concerns us here.

It's about *speed*. Uniformitarianism is a scientific doctrine that assumes that rates of natural processes are the same today as they were in the past. Erosion, deposition, precipitation, natural selection, fire, plate tectonics, radioactive decay, incidental solar radiation. Humans fit right in. For millennia, the human race was content to travel at three miles per hour, read one Sunday *New York Times* in a lifetime, sail across the sea at 10 miles per hour, build stone houses over the course of several generations, paint chapels in four years, and construct 400-foot tall pyramids in 30 years - true, it was for incarnations of the Sun God Horus, who maintained cosmic order, balance, and justice, but the entire dynasty of Sun Gods died at the hands of natural selection, which brought order, balance, and justice by punishing the gods for generations of licentious inbreeding. That was then.

Today, we no longer stroll. Think of the time-saving conveniences we have today: Washing machines, dishwashers, trash compactors, automobiles, electronic garage doors, blow dryers, jet airplanes, and bullet trains. It doesn't end there. Wood processors replaced the axe and compound saw, increasing timber output. Cattle are fed antibiotics to speed up weight gain. Rather than wait for minerals to be exposed at the surface by natural forces, man burrows underground to reach them. Rather than wait for natural disturbances to occur in a forest, we create large, unnatural disturbances at a much faster rate. And, as mentioned, like children running across a busy interstate highway to get to the swimming hole, we take dangerous shortcuts across natural selection.

How fast can we run? Someday, we may see cattle that are spliced with petroleum-eating bacteria, enabling the cattle to eat crude oil, thereby bypassing the time-consuming, petroleum-rich steps from the oilfield, to fertilizer, to cornfield, to corn, to feedlot, to the hybrid cow. One study showed that it takes about 29% more energy to produce a gallon of ethanol than the energy *in* a gallon of ethanol.[3] We can fix that. Skip the plows, sprayers, silos, feedlots, and hired hands with mouths to feed. Speed directly from the oilfield to your calf's four groaning stomachs in one sleek tractor-trailer.

We aren't running, we are time traveling. There is concern about the speed at which data is multiplying. Exponential is the word. The quantity of data produced in 2012 and 2013 exceeded all data produced in the previous years of human existence.[4] Global scientific knowledge increased at about 8-9% in 2012, thus doubling every nine years.[5,6] Currently, digital information is doubling every two to three years. The concern is that "we are overwhelmed with data, making the ability to store, process, analyze, interpret, consume, and act upon that data" uncertain.[7] Like a car traveling faster than the speed of light, it is absolute darkness in front of us and we have no time to react to that deer of infinite mass in the middle of the road.

But we exist outside of virtual reality. In the pre-industrial world, people migrated at roughly the same pace as animals, thus, many components of an ecosystem - seeds, bacteria, insects - were able to migrate along with the prime vector. Ecosystems could assimilate biota at this dispersal rate and range. It is different today. At any given moment there are 10,000 planes in the air, ferrying 1.3 million people from ecosystem to ecosystem at about 500 miles per hour, carrying with them bacteria, fungi, viruses, seeds, insects, reptiles, and mammals. They land in the foreign capital, open their suitcases and out pours a Pandora's Box of howling creatures, out through the window and into the countryside. Mediterranean fruit flies, brown tree snakes, West Nile Virus. Just as data rate and range has exceeded our ability to assimilate, so too, the capacity of ecosystems to absorb foreign biota has been exceeded. When overloaded, computers and networks crash, and they end up in a recycling center along a foamy, foul river in a Third World valley choked with dioxin smoke. Overload an ecosystem with foreign species and the populations of these species explode. The old ecosystem dies, and an alien ecosystem is born.

What we hurriedly bring to birth, a swarm of creations beyond our ability to store, process, analyze, interpret, and consume, is unnervingly familiar, like Dr. Frankenstein's eight-foot-tall creation. Something is not right. It looks like a man, but we wonder why, instead of eating the bowl of stew as all men should, *it is bending the bars of its cage.*

Out he goes. The doctrine of uniformitarianism allows for the occasional catastrophe to accelerate rates of natural processes, events like asteroids, supervolcanoes, gamma-ray bursts, and earthquakes. Humans, having accelerated ozone depletion, carbon emissions, radiation, erosion, deposition, drought, flood, fire, are a twenty-thousand-foot-tall, polystyrene man-shape, escaped from its cage, raining terror upon villages around the globe. We are a god, we have become *Catastrophe*, the destroyer of worlds.

1. *The Curse of the Fly*. Directed by Don Sharp. United States: 20th Century Fox, 1965.

2. *The Fly*. Directed by Kurt Neumann. United States: 20th Century Fox, 1957.

3. David Pimentel, "Ethanol Fuels: Energy Balance, Economics, and Environmental Impacts Are Negative," *Natural Resources Research,* 12(2) (2003): 127–134

4. Åse Dragland, "Big Data, for better or worse: 90% of world's data generated over last two years," SINTEF, Trondheim, Norway, May 22, 2013, https://www.sintef.no/en/latest-news/big-data-for-better-or-worse/

5. Lutz Bornmann and Ruediger Mutz, "Growth rates of modern science: A bibliometric analysis based on the number of publications and cited references," *Journal of the Association for Information Science and Technology,* 66(11 (2015).

6. Richard Van Noorden, "Global scientific output doubles every nine years," Nature Newsblog, May 7, 2014, http://blogs.nature.com/news/2014/05/global-scientific-output-doubles-every-nine-years.html

76. Editorial Team, "The Exponential Growth of Data," Inside Big Data, February 16, 2016, https://insidebigdata.com/2017/02/16/the-exponential-growth-of-data

Chapter 9: Maximum Sustained Yield

One of the early applications of methamphetamine was in warfare. Amphetamines were used in the 1930's during the Spanish Civil War. Use of the drug accelerated during the Second World War when it was administered to soldiers on both sides of the battlefield. Wartime use continued through Korea, Viet Nam, the Second Gulf War, and they continue to be used today.[1] Soon after its discovery, chemists found that methamphetamine relieved sinus congestion and fatigue, enabling humans to exceed normal physical and mental limitations. As often happens when a new scientific truth is born, it is taken from its parents and rushed over to the military laboratory to undergo experiments. Applied to the battlefield it enabled soldiers to work longer and harder, while increasing confidence, aggression, and morale. Thus, maximum battlefield productivity was achieved. During their stunning invasion of France in 1940, Wehrmacht soldiers downed 35 million doses of *Pervitin*, the German brand name for methamphetamine, also called "pilot pills", "panzer chocolate" and "stuka tablets."[2] About 70 million amphetamine pills were issued to British soldiers, about 100 million were available to American soldiers. Japan had similar figures.

Thus, historians should have named it *PED War II*. What might have been if drugs hadn't fueled the soldiers? Maybe everyone would have overslept and 1939 would have passed peacefully.

Since then, the major battlefields have shifted to corporate territory and, as a result, there have been reams of studies and articles about maximizing employee productivity. Expand the market share. Counter the hostile takeover. Erect trade barriers. Defend the intellectual property. The workforce is drilled in the glories of standing meetings, self-care, cultural fit, autonomy, core competency, ideate, incentivize, deep dive, impactful, hyper-local, move the needle, headshot. Yes, to maximize key metrics for cross-functional accountability partners in a co-oriented environment and all that and, we might add, petrichor, umami, coxcomb, Bronze John, apoplexy, chalkstones, grippe, ague, banjanxed, and dandiprat. Somewhere, under the cloak of that verbal fog, we fear the boss is handing out methamphetamines.

The stated objective of this prattle is humanizing the workforce. This might not sit well with Adam Smith, who said profit was the prime objective, not humanization. His theory stated that self-interest would necessarily result in the elevation of the community that surrounds the profiteer; hence self-interest is actually an interest in non-self. That is to say, Blue Johnny's bartender is actually looking out for Blue Johnny as he gets banjanxed, or is it humanized. This leads us to another buzzword aside from the word buzzword: counter-intuitive, which seems suspiciously similar to the word contradiction.

More buzzwords. *Carrying capacity* is the maximum population that an ecosystem can sustain without degrading or destroying the environment. As applied to cattle grazing, the number of cattle released to graze on a grassland is the stocking rate. The carrying capacity is where the stocking rate is the maximum number of cattle that can be released to graze on the grassland without damaging the grassland.

Maximum sustained yield is a resource management strategy that achieves maximum harvest while maintaining the maximum growth rate of the population. As applied to fishery and herd management, a quantity of a species is harvested that reduces the population to a level where a maximum number of individuals will be reproduced to replace the harvested species. Maximum reproductive rates were believed to be at half the carrying capacity of an environment. As applied to forestry, a volume of timber is harvested that matches the maximum volume of timber that can be replaced by growth in that stand of timber.

The carrying capacity for cattle had been determined by forage production, water supply, animal intake, range type, precipitation, topography, time of sampling, plant species, and other grazing animals present in the environment. The maximum sustained yield of a fishery or herd had been determined by forage, population size, distribution, and reproductive rate. The maximum sustained yield of a forest had been determined by species, yield rate, desired commodity, loss due to fire, insects, blowdown, and disease, and other factors.

We repeat ourselves, that is, we say the same things over again. There was a time that medical science thought the human temperament was determined by the balance of *Four Humours*, or fluids, in the human body: blood, black bile, yellow bile, and phlegm, which were expressed in personalities that were sanguine, choleric, melancholic, and phlegmatic. We clear our throat: Not all that is simple is true.

Theories such as these were popular because they were simple and symmetric. So too, with Maximum Sustained Yield and Carrying Capacities. As these theories were applied and the results came in, the analysis revealed that they were oversimplifications. The environment was far more complex. More research was needed. The science did not take into account...the ability of a reduced population to compete with other species, the ecosystem nature of the species and its surroundings, the functional values of mature specimens, the dependence of a population upon byproducts of itself, the genetics or fitness of the specimens harvested, incidental harvest, the life stage of harvested specimens, the loss of virgin specimens, change in genetics of the population, bias toward harvest of fittest specimens, errors in population size and distribution estimates, gene flow between subpopulations, genotype variations, variations in growth rate, impact of climate change on population vitality, natural changes in ecosystem location and attributes, effects on the ecosystem by increases in non-harvested species, niche competition, spatial variability in productivity, edge-of-range effects, impacts of hybrid or genetically modified harvest species, impacts of alien invasive species, and this is really embarrassing.

This problem could be explained by the relatively insignificant man, Grant Williams, who, in 1957, found himself in a quandary: He was shrinking badly, the effect of a mysterious mist and pesticides. The shrinking altered his consciousness. As he slipped through the tiny holes in a window screen, he came to the conclusion that he had learned the "the answer to the riddle of the infinite," that the "unbelievably small and the unbelievably vast eventually meet like a giant circle," and he was on the adventure of a lifetime.[3] With thoughts like that, he wasn't far from nothingness. There is a lesson here for all of us: This realization occurred when he believed that he was half the size of a no-see-um, which would have reduced his grey matter to about 0.00000008% of the volume of an ordinary human brain, barely enough to house fifty thousand neurons and certainly not able to produce abstract thought. This is equivalent to the abstract thinking ability of a boll weevil or a mid-level manager on methamphetamines. So, we are forced to suspend any conclusion; we have insufficient data. There is no record that Mr. Williams admitted himself into a substance abuse facility before his passing in 1985.

We are no better off than Mr. Williams. The list of unaccounted factors is certain to increase as scientific discovery inflates the vastness of ignorance toward a greater infinity, as it comes to know yet another factor it did not know that is connected to a thousand unknowns, ever-shrinking details in an expanding universe of fact. Ignorance is like a hole in the ground: the more you take from it, the bigger it gets. How big? Every bit of knowledge we add increases what we don't know by a factor of, well, X.

While the application of these theories led to the collapse of the Atlantic tuna population, the clearing of old-growth forests, a decrease in upland game birds, the explosion of niche competitors, the loss of outlier populations, to name a few, a management scheme that brings some species and ecosystems nearer to a collapse, a scheme mounted on shaky assumptions and gaping holes in knowledge, such is not the fundamental problem. In each of these applications, the objective is to extract as much as is as possible from the environment. Thus, the problem is deeper than maximizing production, it's the willingness to maximize production. It's how humans think. As land managers, it is part of our corporate culture.

So, while humans don't administer methamphetamines to southern yellow pine, beef cattle, turkeys, grain belt soils, salmon, and other employs, the intent is to extract as much as possible from the environment, which involves pushing it to its physical limits, even beyond its physical limits if there is some scientific discovery that makes it possible. Thus, grasslands are stocked to carrying capacity with cattle that are hundreds of pounds heavier than they were decades ago, thanks to antibiotics, genetics, and growth-inducing drugs. Atlantic salmon have been genetically modified with genes from Pacific salmon and ocean pout so that they grow all year long, about twice as fast as their predecessor. Loblolly pines have been bred to grow 4 times faster than their ancestors did 50 years ago. Prairie soils are sterilized with pesticides and herbicides and fortified with synthetic fertilizers, helping to increase corn production from 26 bushels per acre in 1936 to 180 bushels per acre today, a 600% increase. Rows of corn were planted 42 inches apart in 1900, today they are planted 30 inches apart, and experiments have been conducted on 15-inch and twin rows.

This is a dilemma. The stated objective of much of this maximum production is to feed the world and anything less would be calamitous and irresponsible. It is the war on hunger. But in the fog of corporate war, the stated objective of feeding others may become indistinguishable from the objective of profit, which proceeds from maximum production. Thus, while feeding Blue Johnny bags of chemical-laced grain is said to be looking out for Blue Johnny's interests, intuition says that the contrary is true.

Back to 1939. Soldiers in WWII who were mustered up on methamphetamines suffered ill effects; many crashed after a few days of use, assaulted their officers, begged relatives and friends for more methamphetamines, committed war crimes, and returned home with an addiction. So too with our environment. Pushing it to the limit, running it at full-bore for generation after generation yields maximum production, but there is another limit not envisioned by management driven by production, which, when reached, is bound to produce bad reactions, crashes, degradations, injuries, and mass death.

A tragedy of war is the tragedy of the commons. This environment we share has become a battlefield. Whether one is a combatant or a civilian enjoined in a war effort, given enough time, the drive would ultimately devolve into self-interest, a struggle for individual survival. At that moment, most will act independently of others. The common good is lost in the heat of battle. The end result is Passchendaele, Marne, Gallipoli, Ypres, Somme, a scorched earth shared by all.

1. David Sulzer, Mark S. Sonders, Nathan W. Poulsen, and Aurelio Galli, "Mechanisms of neurotransmitter release by amphetamines: A review," *Progress in Neurobiology* 75 (2005): 406–433.

2. Norman Ohler, *Blitzed - Drugs in the Third Reich* (Boston, MA: Houghton Mifflin Harcourt, 2017).

3. *The Incredible Shrinking Man.* Directed by Jack Arnold. United States: Universal Pictures, 1957.

Chapter 10: Toxic Noise

 Most children are well aware that there is something hiding beneath their bed. Some large, dark shape, breathing slowly, that is poised to grab any limb that dangles over the edge of the bed and pull it under. This is why they are wise to hide beneath the covers. It won't see them, and they won't see it and it will go away and they can fall into a deep sleep, where their dreams will be haunted by more large, dark shapes, breathing slowly, poised to grab any limbs that dangle over the edge.

In the year 1710, a grown adult, George Berkeley, proposed the idea that if a person does not sense something, its existence is not provable. He wrote, "The objects of sense exist only when they are perceived: The trees, therefore, are in the garden...no longer than while there is somebody by to perceive them."[1] Evidently, he was one of those who never outgrew the habit of hiding under the covers. His words resonated with other light sleepers and, in June 1883, *The Chautauquan*, rephrased it, "If a tree were to fall on an island where there were no human beings, would there be any sound?"[2] That vapid phrase survives to this day.

Two months later, on August 27, there was a sound that most people on earth could have heard or felt. There were three explosions on the island of Krakatoa, the third of which was so loud that it was heard 2000 miles away in Perth, Australia and 3000 miles away on the island of Rodrigues in the Indian Ocean. The sound waves from the explosion reached 310 decibels and swept across the globe three and one-half times. The sound ruptured eardrums 40 miles away and deafened anyone within ten miles.

While the monsters under the bed and trees are alleged to disappear when one closes one's eyes, were one to put it out of sight and mind in a landfill, it would not disappear. Evidently, it would remain for millennia. On June 25 of the year after Krakatoa, while in Rome excavating Esquiline, a collapsing, 2000-year-old garbage dump 400 feet from the embankment of Servius Tullius, archaeologist Rodolfo Lanciani had to back away from the ancient dump, which included household waste from one million people and at least 24,000 corpses. He said, "I was obliged to relieve my gang of workmen from time to time, because the smell from that polluted ground (turned up after a putrefaction of twenty centuries) was absolutely unbearable even for men so hardened to every sort of hardship as my excavators."[3]

That kid scares me.

Archaeologist William L. Rathje was familiar with that odor. Starting in the 1970's, he spent two decades excavating nine modern-day landfills. This was not out of desperation, it was his livelihood, he had mouths to feed. He wrote, "Landfills seem to be far more apt to preserve their contents for posterity than to transform them into humus or mulch." Indeed, he found intact, perfectly legible newspapers dating to the 1950's, a fifteen-year-old steak, still recognizable, "in a lot better condition than Ramses II", and, in every excavation he conducted, he found whole hot dogs, some of which were several decades old.[4]

When the ancient Romans buried the ghastly waste at Esquiline under a deep layer of soil, they thought they had made it disappear forever. Horace even wrote a poem about it:

Nunc licet Esquiliis habitare salubribus atque
aggere in aprico spatiari, quo modo tristes
albis informem spectabant ossibus agrum[5]

Translated into English, he said:

But now, one may well live on the Esquiline quite free from pest,
And take a walk upon a sunny terrace, where but a few days ago
The melancholy passersby beheld the fields disfigured by men's
whitening bones.[6]

I'm back.

Obviously, Horace neglected to conduct a long-term environmental impact analysis. Surprise. Two thousand years later, the dead were still there, vigorously exhaling their malignant, pestilential breath. Fifty-five feet below the surface of the earth was as close as they would get to any mythic Roman Underworld, another doctrine that would do well in a landfill, but the problem is that it *is* the landfill and therefore, the problem is compounded. The simple reason is biodegradation does not prosper without light, oxygen, heat, and water.

The doctrine may be called *Phenomenalism*, the belief that things don't exist outside of perception. The fallen tree in the forest, the monster under the bed, the monsters under a blanket of fresh dirt. The Age of Reason was supposed to take care of these superstitions, but it appears that this one slipped through. The faithful are not limited to children or adults shivering under the covers, landfill operators, or Horace the satirist; it includes most of humanity today.

The person throwing a beer can out the window of a car, the fisherman tossing an old fishing net into the ocean, the municipality sending raw sewerage down the river, the bulldozer operator moving dirt over the mounds of shredded plastic, the nations dumping 28,500 barrels of radioactive waste into the Atlantic Ocean 250 miles west of Land's End, and soldiers driving thousands of tons of military equipment into the Pacific Ocean off of the coast of Espiritu Santo Island after World War II, these are faithful acts of Phenomenalism, where sins are absolved by interment. Out of sight, out of mind.

Despite rusting military equipment on some of the beaches, there are beautiful photographs of Espiritu Santo Island, showing a wild desert coastline, perfect for snorkeling and kayaking. There are millions of photographs taken each year of natural sights, carefully framed to exclude trash and marks of civilization. But what were the sounds when these photos were taken? Some of the most photogenic vistas known are backed by urban infrastructure, often roads or concession stands. We do not hear the noise when we marvel at the photo of the natural wonder. This leads us to three corollaries to the doctrine of Phenomenalism. The silence of film has made it easy for humans to believe, "If I don't hear it, it doesn't exist", "Hearing is believing", or worse yet, "If it is sound, it is not trash."

Sound was an unanticipated danger of urbanization. As we explore our soundscape, we are finding a rising decibel level around the world: multimedia players, heavy equipment, street festivals, traffic, airplanes, sporting events, railroads, smokestacks, dogs, and weaponry. We also find a rising level of hearing-impaired

Ignore the man behind the camera.

wildlife, with increased stress, site abandonment, hearing loss, altered communication strategies, altered migration, reproductive failure, missed environmental cues, and the likes. We would do well to take note of the loss, but it's getting harder to pick out the voices in a noisy room and those high notes are totally gone and do I have to shout and maybe I will just get up and go to another room and what? and how many times do I have to tell you to turn up the confounded television? *Do you hear me?* Should this continue to increase, we may not know the difference between a still photograph and reality.

At that point, we might think that the problem of noise has been solved, but we should recall Mr. Lanciani's exciting day. Disappearance is a state of mind. Sifting through our doctrines brings surprises, some very foul, some very loud. We need to dump them into some deep, dark, biologically active pit. The Underworld, Hades. Do it right or years from now they will erupt, rising from the grave, deafening, malignant, pestilential, exhaling the stench of death.

1. George Berkeley, *A Treatise Concerning the Principles of Human Knowledge* (Philadelphia: J. B. Lippincott and Co., 1874), 218.

2. Theodore L. Flood, "The Editor's Table," *The Chautauquan.* June 1883, Volume III, No. 9, 544.

3. Roldolfo A. Lanciani, *Ancient Rome in the light of recent discoveries* (Cambridge, MA: The Riverside Press, 1888), 67.

4. William L. Rathje, *Rubbish! The Archaeology of Garbage* (New York: Harper Collins, 1992), 112-113.

5. Horace. 33BCE. Satires. Satire VIII.

6. R. M. Millington, *A Rhythmical Translation of the First Book of the Satires of Horace. Longman's* (London: Green, Reader, and Dyer, 1869)

Chapter 11: Lost Art

A baby can't draw. A child draws the human form using four straight lines and a circle. An adult art student draws the human form using an assemblage of overlapping circles or ovals; three large ovals describe the torso, four ovals describe a leg, one describes the head, and so forth. Both renditions work as approximations, but always, upon closer inspection, the renditions fail to describe what is seen. The common human head is not a circle, at least at pressures found below 40,000 feet. Besides, the drawings are two dimensional and humans are historically three dimensional and in recent years, it has been argued that we have expanded so greatly that we need to find a fourth dimension to contain us.

Crop circles, Kansas. Image: USDA FSA

It's a fact, humans have an affinity for simple geometric shapes. Lines, triangles, squares, cubes, spheres. It begins in childhood, with shiny silver balls, stick figures, and alphabet blocks. It continues into adulthood, the same simple shapes defining cityscapes, architecture, gardening, interior decorating, sports, prints, storage, cooking, infrastructure, spatial reference systems, raster images, packaging, modern art, it's everywhere you look. The only exception to this seems to be gerrymandered districts, which, despite origins in human geographic design and idealized political thought, exhibit a strikingly random, organic, almost serpentine shape. Of course, this was not the predicted outcome.

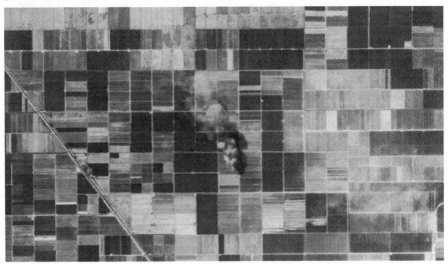

Sugar cane fields, Florida. Image: USGS

Spatial reference systems project grids on the surface of the earth, subdividing it into zones. In 1796, the United States passed an act that ordered the subdivision of the land surface into grids called townships, six miles on each side, containing 36 one-square-mile (640 acres) sections. This is known as the Public Land Survey System (PLSS). This was strictly geometric. It was superimposed on the natural landscape. The organic structure of the environment was ignored, the shapes of floodplains, streams, watersheds, divides, fire perimeters, animal herds, blowdowns, old growth, peatlands, sand barrens, savannas, badlands, and the likes, all seemingly random, irregular polygons.

This comprehension of undeveloped land became a template for city planning, railways, agriculture, waterways, forestry, roads, and even parklands. Human geometry multiplied, like salt crystals in evaporation ponds, superimposed upon the natural environment. This has been romanticized as the taming of nature, the quaint "patchwork quilt" of agriculture, but the consequences are well known: loss of migration corridors, genetic isolation, wetland destruction, channelization, increase of edge species, invasive corridors, loss of interior species, increased blowdown, you name it.

Henry V. Hubbard, Professor of Landscape Architecture at Harvard University stated it this way: "The mature man who has dealt all his life with straight lines, simple surfaces, rigid materials to which he can give permanently almost any form, is likely to attempt something unfitting when dealing with undulating topography, flowing water, and growing plants."[1]

Inside the box. Quito, Ecuador, 2012.

Pie Goes on to Infinity

The PLSS surveyors eventually realized that land on the Mississippi Delta is different from land in the Cascade Range. If you were to purchase a section of land in the delta, it would measure about 640 acres. The topography is geographically flat. That land in the Cascades, it's montane, with an undulating surface. Flattening out the entire surface in the Cascades would result in far more than 640 acres - especially if that section of land was perfectly vertical. That's a lot of grass to mow, but it gets easier once you escape gravity and you find that your head really is a perfect sphere. It also depends upon what scale the flattening would occur. In theory, the scale descends infinitely, so the parcel could contain an infinite acreage, in which case, you have become the greatest feudal lord in the universe. Of course, the same is true for all of the earth's surface, so all landlords are suddenly superior to each other.

The same is true with pie. When it is time for dessert, children fight over the larger piece of the pie. Invariably, one slice is larger than the other, resulting in a bitter dispute. This daily inequality in family food distribution instills a compounding sense of outrage in the children. One parent solved this by having one child cut the slices for the other child. This led to a meticulous, time-consuming effort by the child to make certain the slices were equal in size. It worked. Family peace returned.

Five iterations of the Koch Snowflake

Ah, but this is all a cynical ruse.

72

Parents well know that most children are not physicists. A magnifying glass would reveal minute differences in size which would lead to more disputes, whereby the pie would cool and harden, losing its appeal. Use of a light microscope would reveal even more differences in size, resulting in more disputes and what may appear to be the spontaneous production of fruit flies. Use of an electron microscope would lead to yet more protracted disputes and shocking mold growth. And, in theory, since scale goes on to infinity, an inspection at the smallest possible level would result in starvation and death. So too, with feudal lords. If they had known about the infinite scale of detail, perhaps feudalism would have disappeared sooner than 1867.

The hungry children suffer at the hands of what are called *Fractals*. These are a class of non-differentiable functions that are iterated; there is no derivative; it is not possible to determine the rate at which the function is changing at any given point. Fractal Dimensions refer to an index or measure of the complexity of patterns. This is expressed as a ratio that compares the change in detail in the pattern as the scale at which it is measured changes. The slice of apple pie, for example. As one descends in detail, the irregularities in the border continue to appear. As Benoit Mandelbrot stated, "As even finer features are taken account of, the measured total length increases."[2] The end result: The pie has an infinite outer edge.

The reason is, fractals exhibit self-similarity, that is, the whole has the same shape as the parts, into infinite detail. It is also called expanding symmetry or unfolding symmetry. This can be compared to Russian nesting dolls, a hall of mirrors, or big fish eating medium fish eating small fish. Thus, no indivisible shape exists from which a derivation can be made.

This had applications beyond the chalkboard. Mandelbrot found that while the irregular shapes in the natural world could not be described in terms of classic Euclidian geometry - our beloved lines, triangles, squares, circles - they could be described in terms of fractal dimensions, or fractals, particularly when randomness was inserted into the function. Thus, fractal functions have been discovered that describe coastlines, clouds, mountain ranges, smoke, trees, ferns, seashells, noise, turbulence, galaxy clustering, vascular systems, river systems, the very things we bury beneath concrete and vinyl monuments to Euclidean geometry.

A determinist view of the math behind nature would reject the notion of randomness, but at our level of cognition, unable to track all particles, motion, and force at all scales of existence, this is the best we have. That butterfly in Brazil may well cause a tornado in Texas, but we will never know.

The middle of nowhere. Computer generated fractal landscape.

Art Is

The probability of finding an adult who draws stick figures is increasing over time. This may be due to the loss of our fractal environment. This is akin to the child who is forced to watch television from birth and, as an adult, has no depth perception. We mention this because we are approaching the point where we confuse stick figures and actual, three-dimensional human beings. The stick-figure drawing will hang in the Louvre, in the spot where Michelangelo's *Dying Slave* used to stand.

Beauty is a debate. Scientists have tried to define the nature of beauty, and, as one might expect, the theories focus on utility, especially as an indicator of health, advantageous genes, and fitness despite the burden of ornamentation. Others say that beauty is a product of sensory bias, that the beauty characteristics fit within the range of what the opposite sex is able to sense - light, sound, smell, taste. Others say it is a product of environmental and physiological constraints. Still others say that it is entirely accidental, that the pairing of preferences and ornamentation are arbitrary, and the traits are not necessarily advantageous. This is not something you would say on a date.

Other than philosophical mutterings and the works of Shakespeare, the randomness of fractals that resulted in shapes that mimic those found in the natural environment may be one of the closest things we have to a definition of beauty.

Early in the past century, the National Park Service (NPS) developed a philosophy of landscape architecture, principles that would govern the development of parks for public access and enjoyment. Their objective was "the one dominant purpose of preserving essential esthetic qualities of their scenery unimpaired as a heritage"[3] to generations to come, "substantially unimpaired by the intrusion of other functions,"[4] the "preeminence of a landscape preservation ethic in the development of natural areas of outstanding value."[5] Hubbard wrote, "The good landscape designer must think in terms of natural beauty and natural expression" and that roads, bridges, and houses "are not there for their own sake, and usually the less they are noticed the better...The National Park designer cannot, of course, design the mountains. But if he is from long and humble study an interpreter of natural beauty, he can present the mountains to the observer effectively." He warned, "The architect often regretfully stops his thinking with the outside of his building because he cannot govern what happens nearby."[6] Principles took precedence, not prototypes.

Thus, applying these principles to buildings, roads, bridges, villages, guardrails, culverts, curbs, campgrounds, signs, and trails, the NPS used native materials, plants, shapes, and colors. The structures and landscaping harmonized with the natural surroundings, matching, blending, appearing as if they grew out of the setting, as if they had been there all along.

Now, *this* is art.

An outcome of such an approach is the reduced visual impression of straight lines, triangles, squares, and circles, the dismissal of Euclid, and an increase in the impression of randomness. A closer inspection of the edge of the buildings, roads, bridges, and culverts may reveal a stochastic edge, wandering aimlessly along the line of sight, an edge that, at the moment, we could describe as a fractal, and certainly something that we may define as beautiful.

We might not know much about art, but we know what we like.

Madison Trailside Museum, Madison Junction, Yellowstone National Park.
Date: 1930. Image: NPS, Public Domain.

Limits to Human Growth

Yet, around the world, National Parks are being surrounded by human activity and development. In many places, the borders of the park are clearly defined by the contrast between development and unspoiled wilderness. The development is often visible from within the park, a visual pollution, degrading the visual resources, the viewshed. In many other places, the parks are being encroached by poachers, squatters, miners, humans seeking to convert the value of beauty into economic value. Elsewhere on earth, park status is rescinded, consciously opening it to exploitation, no longer managing for beauty, but for profit. This is a pandemic, an illness of humans sweeping the globe, one that appears when humans are or believe they are threatened by economic failure. This is to say, parklands express a belief in economic security. This is not a sustainable relationship.

So, we return to kindergarten, drawing stick figures all over the place with grease pencils, mesmerized by silver balls, randomly stacking up alphabet blocks into senseless strings of babble. We are fighting over a piece of pie, but this one will not go on forever, despite the geometry, and any more fighting and the whole pie will rot, and nobody gets to eat.

Clear-cuts up to the boundary of Redwoods State and National Parks, CA.
Image: USDA FSA

1. Henry V. Hubbard, "The Designer in National Parks," in *National Park Service, 1941 Yearbook: Park and Recreation Progress* (Washington, DC: US Government Printing Office, 1941), 38-39

2. Benoit Mandelbrot, "How Long Is the Coast of Britain? Statistical Self-Similarity and Fractional Dimension," *Science* 156(3775) (1967), 636

3. Frederick Law Olmstead Jr., "The Distinction between National Parks and National Forests," *Landscape Architecture* 6 (3) (1916): 115, 116.

4. Frederick Law Olmstead Jr., "Vacation in the National Parks and Forests," *Landscape Architecture* 12 (2) (1922): 108.

5. Linda Flint McLelland, *Building the National Parks: Historic Landscape Design and Construction* (Baltimore, MD: The John Hopkins University Press, 1998), 9.

6. Hubbard, "The Designer," 39.

Chapter 12: Save the Economies!

On February 7, 1968, as the war raged in Viet Nam, *New York Times* columnist James Reston stated, "How do we win by military force without destroying what we are trying to save?"[1] The next day, reporter Peter Arnett furnished a famous quote about a battle for Ben Tre to the same newspaper: "It became necessary to destroy the town to save it."[2] Ah, the means are justified by the ends. The process is the product. The medium is the message. These are axioms.

We once sailed at the speed of wind; we now fly beyond the speed of sound. This creates the illusion of a smaller world; the other side of the world is just one lost day away, as we squirm all folded up like origami into a tiny airplane seat gnawing on stale pretzels, but we take comfort in the fact that the scurvy, beriberi, typhus, and fluxes do not plague the passengers or the crew as they did four hundred years ago. One thing remains, though. It is said that the Spanish sailors seeking precious metals in new lands, upon entering the calm, hot, and hazy subtropical zone known as the horse latitudes found it necessary to jettison their stock animals in order to conserve their dwindling supply of fresh water. Today, as we sail along toward global wealth, the natural world is being depopulated, a mass expulsion, just like animals tossed overboard in the horse latitudes. Their carcasses stretch to the horizon, a line of unnumbered species, victims of the Sixth Extinction, the Anthropocene, bobbing in the polymeric sea that boils beneath an angry, setting sun.

The global list of imperiled species is long one; possibly a million are expected to disappear in the next generation.[3] Yet, as these flesh and blood specimens drift to the seabed, taking their place alongside discarded cans of processed lunchmeat and shipping containers filled with rubber ducks, and grieving biologists monitor their descent through census and survey, other investigators spend countless hours fretting over the life of another organism, the one that was instrumental in bringing about the demise of these imperiled species. And its prospects are bleak.

It might sound as if this were referring to the human race, whose decisions have brought about this current extinction crisis, and who are anticipating their turn to appear on the list of imperiled species, a consequence of their profligacy, but it is not. This concerns *The Economy*.

Once Upon a Time

Many have heard an old fable about The Economy. It has been told and retold for generations. It goes something like this:

All around the world, economies are in steep decline, and without immediate action they may disappear altogether. "Unless we intervene soon, we might as well call ourselves economic historians," said Loef Treewelder, chief statistician of the Worldlike Fiduciary Institute. "We will only see them in museums."

In undeveloped lands, economies are disappearing at an alarming rate, and this has begun to spread to developing lands. Economists fear that it threatens the developed world. Treewelder warns, "Western lands may be the last sanctuary of the economy. It may be their last stand. We need to do something now."

A momentum builds when economies start disappearing, a phenomenon economists call "fiscal cascade." When one economy disappears, it removes a source of raw materials, wealth, goods, and services for other economies. This starves the other economies, restricting their resources, taxing their local environments beyond their ability to sustain. The neighboring economies weaken without these resources, and without alternatives, they are pushed toward stagnation, recession, depression, and failure. This, in turn, pressures their neighboring economies to collapse. "It is a cascade," says Treewelder.

"It is like the shock wave of an atomic blast, taking down buildings in ever-widening concentric rings."

For economic populations to thrive there must be sufficient numbers to maintain the viability of the populations. "You cannot sustain vigorous economies without sheer numbers. Drop them below a threshold, and the economies cannot interact, they become isolated, and there are no spin-offs, no further generations, no new-and-exciting products. They start to topple like dominoes. In the end, the economy resorts to auto-cannibalization. Eating the seed stock. You get salesmen selling to family members. Grocers looting their own grocery. The auto mechanic slashes brake lines on his brother's car, doctors get high on their own prescriptions. It gets ugly. It is something you would not want to see."

What has happened in the developing lands may portend how developed lands would collapse. Treewelder continues, "The economy in those regions gobbled up all of its resources. The land is stripped bare, and all you have left are empty markets and mobs of hungry people raiding empty stalls. Soon they will be raiding each other. 'I will take your watch if you take my hat.' That sort of thing. This is our future."

Inflation, says Treewelder, is often misinterpreted. "We usually think in terms of supply and demand, but that is only true in a whole environment. But in a degraded, disassembled, or decomposed environment, such as we have crafted in these modern times, supply and demand are overwhelmed by resource scarcity. This leads to inflationary pressures. I liken it to the swelling of limbs you see in congestive heart failure. This doesn't mean that the person is increasing in stature, he is not becoming larger than life, no, it means his heart is dying."

The size of economies today has increased, placing greater pressure on raw materials and finished goods. Helmikt Dredspukette, of the Brainoverbinge Fund, observes, "We used to have these little, village-based economies where a collapse wouldn't be noted outside of the local barbershop or tavern. Villages over the range or across the river carried along as if nothing was amiss. 'I hear the village over the hill burned down,' they would say, and play another round of *Bubble the Justice.* Today, the economies are so large, so integrated, and so voracious that feeding them the resources necessary to keep them alive is daunting. Our grandparents had no idea that their grandchildren would be shoveling billions of their quaint little inventions - the locomotive, the horseless carriage, the moving picture show, the flying machine, the television box - into the mouth of an insatiable colossus, our modern economy. When we run out of those, we start shoveling our children into its mouth."

And then there is the need for corridors. Dredspukette states, "The modern economy is so large and singular within a given land mass, that it has far fewer economies with which to interact than in the past. This requires large-scale corridors over which the economy can traverse and contact others of its kind. Sadly, many of these avenues are blocked by fears, superstitions, prejudices, greed, deception, and self-interest, and lately, environmental protectionism. This is a quandary; while preventing economic interrelationships, they are in fact, the very conditions upon which the individual economy thrives. The solution creates the problem. That's a glitch. We are looking into that right now."

Solutions

And that they are. Economists are looking for answers wherever they can be found. Some are probing the underpinnings of the modern economy for an answer. Ambler O'Schmidlerz, chief strategist for Tricycle Investment Group looks to the 18th century. "Adam Smith, in his work, *The Wealth of Nations*, gave us the guiding principle," he contends. "He spoke of the 'invisible hand' of self-interest, the profit motive, if you will, that unintentionally produces a collective good for society. This was sheer genius. Like the man who builds a tower for his grain that happens to give shade to the homeless people. *So what* if they are homeless because he took over their land? Or they can't afford the grain? They still benefit, don't they? It's like burning down a village to save it. We can all sleep with a good conscience, knowing the homeless people are resting in the shadow of what used to be their homes." He closes his eyes. "We need to return to this simple stratagem."

O'Schmidlerz continues, "But we need to invoke the invisible hand with more vigor than promoting self-interest. We need to create consumer confidence. Confidence in what? Not in resources, corridors, interactions. No, we must recreate the belief in *the economy*, the belief that the economy continues to thrive for the economy to continue to thrive."

He shifts his weight and adjusts his suspenders. "Wealth is largely the conviction of wealth - and it is relative at that. Picture the wealthy

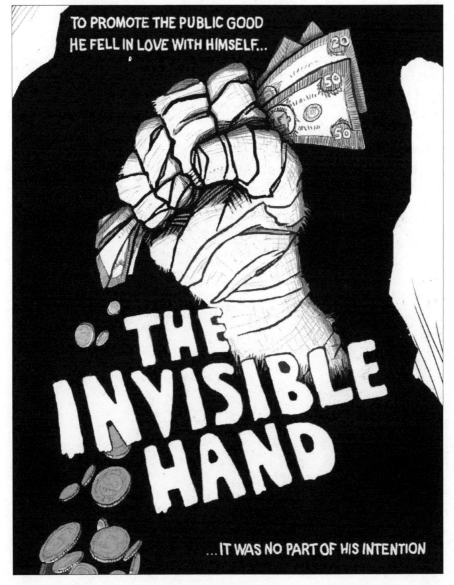

TO PROMOTE THE PUBLIC GOOD
HE FELL IN LOVE WITH HIMSELF...

THE INVISIBLE HAND

...IT WAS NO PART OF HIS INTENTION

man in Borneo and compare him to the wealthy man in Lichtenstein. There is no comparison, yet each parts crowds of patrons at the best restaurant in town with a flip of his wrist. The man in Borneo imagines himself wealthy although he possesses a few stone wheels and seashells. We need to convince people that they are prosperous, regardless of their prosperity. Children are enamored with plastic jewelry. People are the same; lavish them with real wealth or imitation wealth, whatever works. The death of the economy will go unnoticed."

He pauses to light up a large cigar. "Besides, the only thing that works in a depleted environment is something akin to catch-and-release fishing; you don't consume anything, just *pretend* you are, then step aside, and let the next fellow do the same." He tips his head back and blows smoke rings. "And, if you happen to be the next fellow in line and you are under the influence of the invisible hand, why, you just take that fish right out of the water and fry it up! *'For humanity!'* you say. Well done! You have done your civic duty; you have produced the collective good. The economy will live to see another day."

Yes, another day, one we will never see, where an invisible hand stalks an empty planet, having saved us all.

1. James Reston, "The Flies That Captured the Flypaper," *New York Times,* February 7, 1968, 46.

2. Peter Arnett, "Major Describes Move," *New York Times,* February 8, 1968, 14.

3. IPBES, *Summary for policymakers of the global assessment report on biodiversity and ecosystem services of the Intergovernmental Science-Policy Platform on Biodiversity and Ecosystem Services.* S. Díaz, J. Settele, E. S. Brondizio E.S., H. T. Ngo, M. Guèze, J. Agard, A. Arneth, P. Balvanera, K. A. Brauman, S. H. M. Butchart, K. M. A. Chan, L. A. Garibaldi, K. Ichii, J. Liu, S. M. Subramanian, G. F. Midgley, P. Miloslavich, Z. Molnár, D. Obura, A. Pfaff, S. Polasky, A. Purvis, J. Razzaque, B. Reyers, R. Roy Chowdhury, Y. J. Shin, I. J. Visseren-Hamakers, K. J. Willis, and C. N. Zayas (eds.) (Bonn, Germany, IPBES secretariat, 2019)

Chapter 13: Exclusion

 Exclosures are plots of land that have barriers that prevent certain species from entering the plot. In western North America, the excluded species are usually domestic grazing animals such as cattle, horses, and sheep. In scientific studies, an exclosure is established as a baseline to which the rest of the surrounding landscape can be compared. This, in turn, shows the effects of grazing or browsing animals upon the environment. In centuries past, the barriers were made of stones and wood, but this changed with the invention and mass production of barbed wire in the late 1800's.

There are many exclosures in western North America. Some examples: The Lamar Exclosure is found in Yellowstone National Park in Wyoming, east of the Lamar Ranger Station on the north side of Lamar Valley. Established in 1957 to restrict shrub browsing by elk and pronghorn antelope, the exclosure saw an increase in diversity, size, and range of shrub species over the decades. Today, the exclosure contains a grove of quaking aspen; only aspen seedlings are found immediately outside of the exclosure. This aspen suppression is attributed to herbivory, the browsing of elk.[1] Then there is the Quinn exclosure, southwest of Quinn, South Dakota on the Buffalo Gap National Grassland. It was set on a north-facing side slope in mixed-grass prairie. Today, the exclosure hosts a thicket of chokecherry, plum, green ash, buffaloberry and other shrubs while outside of the exclosure, where cattle graze, grasses and forbs dominate, and few shrubs are found. Another is the Flagstaff Exclosure. It is on the Lewis and Clark National Forest south of Checkerboard, Montana, in the Castle Mountains. Dense tufts of rough fescue comprise 50% of the cover in this exclosure while outside of the exclosure, where cattle graze, rough fescue comprises only 6% of the cover. This is a recurring theme.

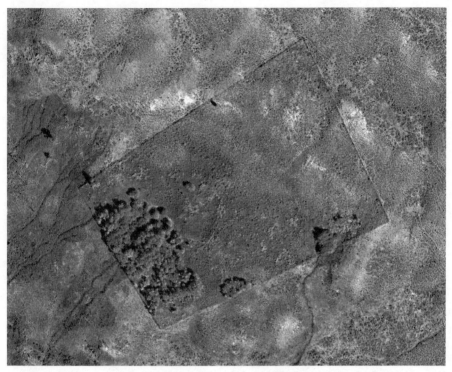

Lamar Exclosure. Source: "Yellowstone" lat 44.885422° lon -110.218596°
Google Earth. 9/11/2015. 4/16/19.

Originally, North America was open range. Herds of wild animals were free to migrate. In the late 1800's, the bison and other ungulates were virtually exterminated and replaced with European cattle. The cattle occupied the bison niche and, at first, were relatively free to migrate, much like the bison. However, as farming operations were established, cattle encroached on the farms and ate the crops. Disputes arose. Farmers and cattlemen fought over land rights. This gave rise to the need for fencing to exclude the cattle. Wood and stones were scarce and expensive, so the relatively inexpensive, newly invented barbed wire was strung across the open range. This conflict simmered for years and many of you may recall that it boiled over on the set of the movie *Oklahoma* when a brutal fistfight erupted between farmers and cowmen, a grisly spectacle made all the more horrific as the bystanders - women, children, and the elderly - heartened the brawlers with festive music and dancing.[2]

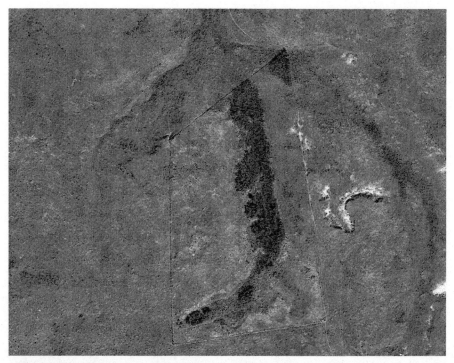

*Quinn Exclosure. Source: "Quinn" lat 43.977814° lon -102.155374°
Google Earth. 9/25/2011. 4/16/19.*

They sang:

*The farmer and the cowman should be friends.
Oh, the farmer and the cowman should be friends.
One man likes to push a plough, the other likes to chase a cow,
But that's no reason why they cain't be friends.*[3]

They should but would not. Now, this fight was not sanctioned by any athletic federation and, as a result, there was no boxing ring. There are three ropes around a boxing ring, much like the wires on a barbed wire fence, however, there are no barbs on the ropes, and none are electrified at this time. Why the ropes? A newcomer to the spectacle might reason that the purpose of the ring is to prevent the boxers from escaping and beating up the people in the audience. Another might reason that it is to keep the audience from storming the ring and beating up the contestants, much like European soccer. So, the fans debate: Which directional movement do the ropes prevent, into the ring or out of the ring?

This helps us to understand where the Louisiana Territory settlement went wrong. Which directional movement do fences prevent? Originally, fences were strung to exclude grazing animals, preventing animals from assaulting the croplands. But this changed with the expansion of agricultural lands; fences were strung to include grazing animals, both wild and domestic. In the case of wild animals, especially bison and pronghorn antelope, they were always included or confined to a relatively small, relatively wild preserve, which prevented humans from assaulting the animals. Thus, the function of the barrier inverted, from exclusion to inclusion, reversing flow like the mighty Chicago River. This has created a plethora of rural zoos across the globe, caged wildlife zones, animal enclaves, where wild animals are not free to migrate and, at best, are managed much like cattle, manually rotated from pasture to pasture or culled when they escape or exceed grazing capacity.

Those two exclosures shown in the photos, they are exclosures within exclosures, really, and they have demonstrated that the animals in the greater exclosure are exceeding the carrying capacity of the land.

Huh. In recent decades, we have observed the ascent of another species that has rapidly exceeded the carrying capacity of the land, expanding its range, population, and consumption at an unsustainable rate, eliminating other species and habitats and degrading ecosystem health. It ranges across all barriers, is found in every partition. We would propose an enclosure for this species, to allow recovery of the remnant ecology and free range of wild animals, but it owns the patent for the barbed wire, and we would expect that the species, finding itself competing for inadequate resources within a confined space, would strike out violently.

1. Pamela G. Sikkink, "Yellowstone Sage Belts 1958 to 2008: 50 Years of Change in the Big Sagebrush (Artemisia tridentata) Communities of Yellowstone National Park," *Natural Resources and Environmental Issues* 17(19) (2011).

2. *Oklahoma!* Directed by Fred Zinneman. United States: Rodgers & Hammerstein Pictures, 1955.

3. Oscar Hammerstein II, *The Farmer and The Cowman* (Williamson Music Company, 1955)

Chapter 14: Ecosystem

A favorite pastime of many a second grader is to find a first grader and trade his nickel for the first-grader's dime. This is easy to do. Here is why:

In America and Canada, the five-cent nickels are larger than the ten-cent dimes. The first grader thinks that the dime is of less value because it is smaller, so he readily gives up his nickel. The second-grader knows that the value is not based on size but it was determined by the content of silver in the coin in comparison to the silver dollar and that value of silver is attributed by supply and demand, global inflation, trade imbalances, central bank activities, interest rates, and other commodity prices and that, in 1866, officials at the United States Mint decided to make the nickel larger than the dime by removing the silver and changing its content to a combination of copper and nickel.

Due to his ignorance of these facts, the first grader does not perceive the nature or value of the dime and squanders it. The second grader makes a 100% profit on every exchange and laughs all the way to the ice cream man. Ah, recess hour was not long enough. The only thing that prevented us from becoming millionaires was the limited supply of first graders.

It is said that there is wisdom with the aged. Yet, adults will readily trade a tallgrass prairie for a neatly arranged corn field with clean, straight rows 24 inches apart. They will trade an old-growth yellow birch and eastern hemlock forest for a lime green golf course with rolling fairways and artificial lakes, a rich fen for a dredged pond with mortared stone shores and a concrete fountain, beech-maple forest for a field of solar panels, a prairie river for a highway, a slickrock canyon for a hydroelectric dam, Sonoran desert for a neon-lit business district, mountains for skyscrapers, a herd of bison for a railroad. This is easy; we already have.

By and large, adults have failed to perceive the nature of our environment. These are exquisite machines, extremely complex systems that have been traded away. They are called *Ecosystems*. A system of ecology, a biological machine, a community of biotic and abiotic components, with processes between them all. Some define ecosystems by region, some by components, some by processes. In all cases, it's a dynamic system, with interactions between the components and constantly changing characteristics. The scale of an ecosystem varies, from large-scale, general systems, such as Grassland Ecosystems, which exist in North America, Eastern Europe, Argentina, and Australia, to detailed, more specific systems, such as Tallgrass Prairie, which exists in the eastern third of the central grasslands province in North America - if you call 4% of the original an existence. That's more

False tendrils, Xalapa, Mexico, 2013.

like a museum piece, like pointing to Martha, the stuffed Passenger Pigeon at the Smithsonian and saying the species still exists. It is far easier for us to perceive the systemic qualities of an airliner, golf course, cornfield, solar farm, interstate highway, business district, or skyscraper than it is for us identify systems in nature. Maybe it is the microscopic scale of the components, or that we take it for granted, or that the processes are often invisible to the naked eye, or we can't recognize when it is breaking or broken.

It does not help that the web of technology that encircles our globe may be confused with an ecosystem. In the information technology industry, the entertainment industry, and economics, the word "ecosystem" has been annexed to describe the network of competition and collaboration between various entities; in the computer industry, this word is used to describe the network of users, rules, hackers, programmers, software, and hardware, and perhaps the employee restroom.

By and large, adults have failed to perceive the value of our environment. For example, that beech-maple forest filled with sugar maple trees has the finest solar panels on earth. We call them "leaves." In the case of sugar maple (*Acer saccharum*), its leaves take that sunlight, those photons, and use it to oxidize water, producing free oxygen, hydrogen, and electrons. Oxygen is tree waste is human treasure. Most of the hydrogen and electrons are transferred to carbon dioxide which is reduced to organic products, most notably, the carbohydrate sugar, which saturates the maple sap in the spring as the tree is sending energy upward to make new leaves, adding nutrients provided by the decay of its own maple leaves shed in previous years. Humans tap that sap, boil off the water, bottle it, and pour it on their pancakes. This is alchemy, turning sunlight into sugar. Other organic products of the leaf include cellulose, which, after cutting, splitting, and drying for a season, will produce 24 million BTU's per cord, which heat can be used to fry those pancakes. Again, this machine doesn't end at the limits of the range of the beech-maple forest; ecosystems are nested, they exist at different scales. The entire earth is one unified ecosystem. So too, the solar system, the galaxy, the universe. We need that gravity as badly as we need oxygen.

By comparison, the solar farm that stands where a beech-maple forest once stood produces electricity through the photovoltaic effect and elicits cheers from trade journals, zoning commissioners, manufacturers, and power companies. The farm is an interconnected grid of photovoltaic solar panels that are composed of silicon, aluminum, cadmium, copper, indium, gallium, selenide, plastic, perovskite, and other materials. In about 30 years, global waste from expired solar panels is estimated to amount to 78 million metric tons.[1] Much of this waste is toxic. Solar panels are not prime habitat for nesting birds, decaying solar panels do not provide nutrients for new solar panels for centuries to come, nor is cutting, splitting, and burning solar panels for heat recommended by manufacturers.

Heavily armed with this ignorance, humans take bold action. There are few people who would fly in an airplane that is being assembled in midflight. Currently, it is said that planes are assembled on the ground before launching them into the vast brown skies. The same can be said about most of the components of an airplane. There are few people who would fly in an airplane whose components are being assembled in midflight - engine, fuel lines, hydraulic system, electronic system, rudders, landing gear. They are constructed on the ground, then assembled as an airplane, then taken to the runway and off they go!

The inverse is true. Only a few *stooges* would fly while dismantling a plane in flight.[2] An airplane is an integrated system, irreducible, and would eventually fail if critical components were not inline and operative while in flight. There is probably some international law that makes it a crime to gut an airplane in midflight, pulling out the copper wires and stainless steel tubes and hoses, selling them for scrap to the highest bidder - that man in seat 18C, dressed in sunglasses, black raincoat, dark suit, black clip-on tie, and mother of pearl tie pin, who keeps on ordering bourbon and soda, the one with the four parachutes. Or to that hairy fellow standing outside on the wing who is trying to tear the cowling from the propeller engine as you cruise at 20,000 feet.

Yet, this is precisely what we are doing. While about 2% of Americans do not believe so, the earth is actually a spheroid hurtling around the sun at 67,000 miles per hour. It is loaded with systems:

electronic, hydraulic, hydrologic, geologic, grassland, oceanic, montane, watershed, decomposition, migration, tidal, weather. As we fly, we are gutting the earth of copper, aluminum, iron, platinum, grass, trees, fish, mammals, ozone, most of it intentional, most of it for profit, and selling it to the highest bidder, that man from seat 18-C who just jumped off of the plane to save his life.

Leave us some oxygen, will you?

We need to educate and protect that first grader. He has no clue what he holds in his hand. But it is clear that he would prefer the tallgrass prairie over a billion cornfields since the prairie has leopard frogs, horned lizards, regal fritillary butterflies, pallid sturgeon, Whooping Cranes, bull snakes, intermittent creeks, spring seeps, plains spadefoot toads, smooth softshell turtles, burying beetles, nematodes, pronghorn antelope, Ferruginous Hawks, hailstorms, spring floods, drought, predators, decomposition, landslides, prairie fires, snowmelt - an infinite number of biotic and abiotic entities and processes which it would take an eternity to list.

1. Stephanie Weckend, Andreas Wade, Garvin Heath. "End-of-Life Management: Solar Photovoltaic Panels." International Renewable Energy Agency (IRENA) and International Energy Agency Photovoltaic Power Systems (IEA-PVPS), Report Number: T12-06:2016, June 2016.

2. *Dizzy Pilots*. Directed by Jules White. United States: Columbia Pictures, 1943.

Chapter 15: Biotic Homogenization

 As an invading army overwhelms an indigenous population, the tradition has been to strip the native peoples of their culture - dress, music, art, food, grooming, language - and compel them to adopt the culture of the invading army. This has been true in one continent after another, particularly during the colonial era. As a result, many indigenous cultures became moribund or extinct, reduced to museum pieces, static, frozen in time like a watch that stopped during an atomic blast.

Extrapolating this historic data leads us to the end of civilization, where humans have attained a singular global culture: one dress, one music, one art, one food, one grooming, and one language. Global uniformity. Homogeneity. We face a monoculture future of tee-shirts, official sports team hats, basketball shoes, commercial art, autotuned pop, fries, hamburgers, a beer, and slang. We shudder. That is something right out of science fiction.

Today, various monitoring systems enable us to observe and measure the demise of ecosystems and their species as they happen. The most comprehensive monitoring arrangement is the Natural Heritage Program, a database developed by The Nature Conservancy and networked at NatureServe that tracks the locations of rare and threatened species and communities for states, provinces, and many countries. The lists of rare species and communities for a given jurisdiction are astonishingly long. New York State, for example, currently lists 349 endangered, 155 threatened, 86 rare, and 153 vulnerable plants. That's 743 plant species in New York alone that are at risk of extirpation or extinction. The list for rare animals is 19 pages long. We did not bother to count, it's like counting rabbits; by the time you get done, you have to start all over again. We are sure that someone has been assigned the task and, if this depopulation continues, his job would become easier if someone would tell him to just count the species that are *not* imperiled.

Multiply this by the world.

One may notice that these lists omit *Homo sapiens*. It might be hard to justify adding them to the list when you see there are some 7.7 billion of them swarming over the surface of the planet, but they persist in not understanding that human existence is bound to the existence of other life on the planet. It's like throwing a horse over the side of a wooden ship while forgetting that you are sitting in the saddle. It is clear, were this trend to continue, eventually we would be on the list, sinking beneath the surface of the unusually hot, flat sea along with the thrashing horses - Przewalski's horses - and polar bears, Magenta Petrel, Saimaa ringed seal, orangutans, and by the way, we just noticed, a raft of about 150 million tons of plastic trash. Where did that come from? A few more decades and that thing could weigh more than all of the fish in the oceans.[1]

MISSING

HAVE YOU SEEN THIS MAN?

Today, a spinning raft of remarks uttered by humans enables us to observe and measure the demise of the human ecological mind as it happens. It has become common to hear the assertion that protecting other creatures on earth is unnecessary, that their value is overestimated, their niche in the ecosystem can be replaced by domesticated, universal species. It is also very common to hear the assertion that the worth of native or rare species or ecosystems is inferior to that of commodities, agriculture, economy, jobs, housing, transportation, and technology. This is current. This is tragic. This is mass self-strangulation, Jonestown, Earth. We have lost sight of the fact that the original ecosystems were what made it possible to have commodities, agriculture, economy, jobs, housing, transportation, and technology. It is like believing that one's parents never existed.

In this mindset, the desired future outcome may be wheat, corn, soybeans, rice, eucalyptus, Kentucky bluegrass, banana trees, palm oil trees, coffee shrubs, and Ring-necked Pheasants. Commodities. These species have been intentional, desired introductions. Other intentional introductions had undesired effects. These included cottontail rabbits, Starlings, kudzu, and a thousand more. Other introductions have been unintentional, spread across the globe by air and ship; waifs, stowaways, and refugees, smuggled in steel shipping containers, wooden pallets, and airplane cargo holds. These include Norway rats, zebra mussels, brown tree snakes, gobi fish, and a million more. Don't ask us to count.

As mentioned in Chapter 8, the rate of introduction is a fundamental problem. High rates of introduction tend to exceed *ecosystem resilience*. Ecosystem resilience is its ability to return to its prior state after a perturbation. When the perturbation is an introduced species, this resilience is usually a function of natural enemies in the invaded ecosystem and the quantity of invading individuals. In the case of Hawaii, the current rate of biological invasions "are nearly one million times higher than the prehistoric rate for Hawaii before human influence."[2] This transport is occurring across the globe, in all latitudes and across regions that had natural barriers to dispersal, such as oceans, mountain ranges, deserts, or ice fields, objects that were essential in maintaining distinct ecosystems. As Charles Darwin observed in 1859, "barriers of any kind, or obstacles to free migration, are related in a close and important manner to differences between the productions of various regions."[3]

This being so, where conditions are favorable, as when there are no natural enemies, the sheer quantity of invaders is high, or where the species propagates quickly and aggressively, these species can rapidly colonize the new territory and in so doing, the introduction becomes an invasion. They are said to have "winning traits." Some have caused severe ecological damage, radically altering the invaded ecosystem, exterminating species as they fill their niche. Emerald ash borer, Asian longhorned beetle, thousand canker disease, hemlock wooly adelgid, spiny water flea, Eurasian water-milfoil, beech scale, brown tree snake, chestnut blight, white-nose syndrome, Dutch elm disease, and we have another tiring list.

In practice then, this composite of alien species that is being introduced with varying degrees of intent around the globe is advancing, threatening to homogenize all regions with similar environmental conditions - precipitation, temperature, soil, geology, insolation, slope, aspect, and such. Similar environments around the globe are displaying increasing numbers of identical species. They are becoming alike. This is called *biotic homogenization*, where "the same non-native species are being introduced to multiple locations" causing "disparate regions to become more similar in their species composition through time," "a broader ecological process by which formerly disparate biotas lose biological distinctiveness at any level of organization, including in their genetic and functional characteristics."[4]

This means war. Like an invading army, humans are conquering the entire earth, colonizing continent after continent, imposing their standardized ecoculture everywhere they plant their flag. Indigenous ecocultures - both their species and functions - are being extirpated. Global uniformity, homogeneity, our ecosystem faces a monoculture future where earth teems with three species of edible plants, a dozen species of farm animals, two household pets, and a few hundred disease-carrying pests that came along for the ride. Poodle habitat!

We reread the rare species list, looking for humans, but they haven't made the list yet. Ah - what were we thinking - when that happens, who would be reading? Most of us would be in museums, anyhow.

1. World Economic Forum, *The New Plastics Economy — Rethinking the future of plastics* (Ellen MacArthur Foundation and McKinsey & Company, 2016), http://www.ellenmacarthurfoundation.org/publications

2. Julian D. Olden, Julie L. Lockwood, and Catherine L. Parr, "Biological Invasions and the Homogenization of Faunas and Floras" in *Conservation Biogeography*, ed. Richard J. Ladle and Robert J. Whittaker (West Sussex UK: Wiley-Blackwell, 2011), 226. DOI:10.1002/9781444390001

3. Charles Darwin, *On the Origin of Species* (Cambridge, MA: Harvard University Press, 1859), 347.

4. Olden, "Biological Invasions," 229-230.

Chapter 16: Emergence

Dawn, erupting. Below is a flock of Sandhill Cranes at the Rowe Sanctuary on the Platte River in Nebraska in early April 2018. This particular morning there were about 70,000 cranes in the flock. At the peak of this migration, there were 650,000 cranes at the sanctuary. This breezy, chilly morning, they were roosting in the river, standing idly on sandbars and sandy shallows squawking to one another.

About an hour after sunrise, the birds at the western end broke ranks and flew. This initiated a wave of bird flight that washed over the entire flock of roosting birds, covering 8,000 feet in two minutes.

This may remind one of an Esther Williams water ballet or a college football card stunt. Maybe it can explain how it is possible that an ordinarily sedate and unremarkable individual, content to knit, nap, and putter with a jigsaw puzzle all day long, can, during a thought-free, summer-evening stroll along the sidewalk down the to the city park, encounter a seething mob and be thoroughly inflamed by fiery speeches about rights, action, and needs and join the mob in a rush toward the business district where he or she hurls dozens of Molotov cocktails at random buildings and loots a burning appliance store. Like these cranes, at dusk, this otherwise unremarkable individual settles into a wingback chair and knits until dawn, occasionally glancing up at the brand-new television and rubbing a torn rotator cuff.

This is how that can be: Regarding great works of architecture, Frank Lloyd Wright once wrote of the "spiritual idea that form and function are one."[1] This is true in the case of the individual crane - or any bird, mammal, fish, reptile, amphibian, insect, or plant, for that matter. They are all at the intersection of science and art, a sweet spot, electrifying the mind and heart.

But once 70,000 individual cranes are aloft, the individual cranes vanish, subsumed into the flock. They cohere, become a unit, and this becomes another entity, a new creature with 70,000 organs. Confined in space, with discreet boundaries, and moving in unison, it behaves like a mile-long cobra, a sprinting cheetah, a Shastriya Nritya dancer, or an angry mob of Molotov cocktail-throwing knitters.

This is called *Emergence*. This organismic property of flocks of birds, schools of fish, herds of animals, and swarms of insects is a property that is not shared with the individual members of the group. It arises or emerges from the interaction of the members. This is one of those constructs where the whole is greater than the sum of the parts. Here, the added energy is from interactions between the parts.

As the science goes, the members of the flock, herd, school, or swarm follow certain rules, namely, Separation, Cohesion, and Alignment.

Separation: They keep a certain distance from one another, like birds on a wire or passengers on a plane flight.

Cohesion: At the same time, they steer toward the average position of their neighbors, keeping a certain closeness to one another, which maintains boundaries and group identity. This we are able to perceive, it is ostensive.

Alignment: Each moves in the same average direction.

Following these rules of interaction, the result is an elevated state, a higher being, the organic shape that moves across the sky like a giant flying snake. In turn, this electrifies humans, who, in turn, feverishly churn out photographs, paintings, grandiose prose, and long-winded, bombast about a lost earth.

Emergent beings were once common in North America. On September 17, 1804, near the confluence of Corvus (American) Creek and the Missouri River, south of Oacoma, South Dakota, an electrified Merriwether Lewis stood on high ground and wrote these words:

This plane extends with the same bredth from the creek below to the distance of near three miles above parrallel with the river, and is intirely occupyed by the burrows of the barking squril hertefore discribed; this anamal appears here in infinite numbers, and the shortness and virdue [verdure] of grass gave the plain the appearance throughout it's whole extent of beatifull bowlinggreen in fine order...a great number of wolves of the small kind, halks and some pole-cats were to be seen...The surrounding country had been birnt about a month before and young grass had now sprung up to hight of 4 Inches presenting the live green of the spring. this senery already rich pleasing and beatiful, was still farther hightened by immence herds of Buffaloe deer Elk and Antelopes which we saw in every direction feeding on the hills and plains. I do not think I exagerate when I estimate the number of Buffaloe which could be compreed at one view to amount to 3000.[2]

A great naturalist, not a spelling bee champion. Again, the numbers vary, but it is estimated that, prior to European settlement, North America had 40 to 60 million bison, 40 million pronghorn antelope, 10 million elk, two million bighorn sheep, one billion prairie dogs, five billion Passenger Pigeons. Today, there are a half-million bison, one million antelope, one million elk, 70 thousand bighorn sheep, 20 million prairie dogs, and no Passenger Pigeons. Similar sharp declines can be shown for American Golden Plover, Red Knot, Sage Grouse, fifteen bat species, wolverines, fishers, pine martens, grizzlies, wolves, and many more.

Imperiled species, thousands of them, are listed with various environmental organizations - Red List, Working List, Natural Heritage Inventory, Endangered Species List. But we find no Emergents on any of these lists. No mention of threatened or extinct herds, flocks, schools, swarms. Resource agencies may refer to "herd management" but rarely does it consider emergent properties. Lowered expectations, apparently. This is not a surprise; when Lewis scanned the horizon, there were no fences, roads, cities, transmission lines, dams, livestock, or croplands to thwart herd, school, swarm, or flock behavior. Emergence hadn't been obstructed.

So it is, as the Sandhill Crane habitat shrinks, and flock behavior is restricted, we don't expect to see the Sandhill Crane Flock make any Red List. Poor things. Good for us they don't know how to make gasoline bombs.

1. Frank Lloyd Wright. *An Autobiography.* New York: Duell, Sloan, and Pearce, 1943, 146.

2. M. Lewis, W. Clark, and Members of the Corps of Discovery, *The Journals of the Lewis and Clark Expedition, Volume 3 August 25, 1804-April 6, 1805.* (G. Moulton, Ed.) (Lincoln, NE: University of Nebraska Press, 2002), 153.

Chapter 17: Cumulative Effects

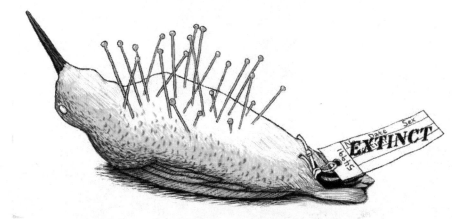

The Code of Federal Regulations, Title 40, Chapter V, Part 1508.7 defines "cumulative impact" as "the impact on the environment which results from the incremental impact of the action when added to other past, present, and reasonably foreseeable future actions...Cumulative impacts can result from individually minor but collectively significant actions taking place over a period of time."[1]

The USGS photo below displays the cumulative effect of a dozen ground-disturbing projects upon a 60-acre parcel of mixed-grass prairie in western North Dakota over the course of 70 years. Roads, pipelines, well pads, fence lines, furrows, borrow pits. It is likely that, as each project came up for consideration, someone determined that the action would have a minor impact on the landscape. But in aggregate, the twelve projects resulted in a major impact upon the landscape; despite reclamation efforts, persistent scars indicate widespread habitat degradation, corridors for invasive species, erosion, failed prairie regeneration, loss of biodiversity, loss of species, loss of original ecosystem components, loss of original ecosystem characteristics, and so forth.

This may bring to mind a tragedy in New York City, 1933.

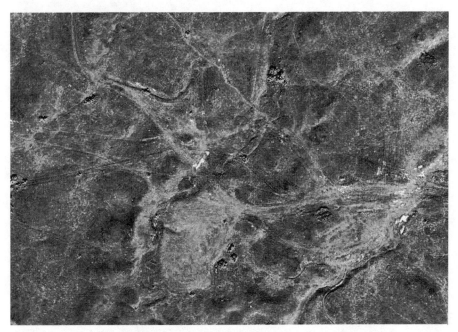

Disturbance scars, McKenzie County, ND. USGS photo.

That year, a 50-foot tall gigantic, semi-humanoid gorilla scaled the Empire State Building and took on modern civilization, swinging his powerful arms at the sky.[2] Four Curtiss F8C-5/O2C-1 Helldivers, a 1920's Marine Corps biplane, swarmed the prehistoric ape and fired upon him with their .303-caliber Lewis guns, two fixed forward firing guns and one flexible rear cockpit gun. While the .303-caliber bullet was designed to kill humans, against a simian of that size, each bullet would be proportional to a .038-caliber bullet fired at a six-foot man. That's about the width of a mechanical pencil lead.

This is impractical. A war fought with mechanical pencil lead would take hundreds of years to wage, reducing, by comparison, the wars between the Kings of England and the Kings of France to a mere border skirmish, and risking, in theory, a rapid descent into world peace. To overcome this disadvantage, Kong was assaulted by four biplanes with a total of 12 Lewis guns for nearly three minutes, firing their guns in seventeen one-second bursts. As many as 170 rounds of ammunition may have penetrated his shimmering latex and rabbit-fur hide. One bullet alone wouldn't kill him, but the cumulative effect of 170 rounds had a significant, lethal impact. Bleeding badly, Kong tumbled from the spire and landed at the intersection of 5th Avenue and West 33rd Street, where a drug store and hair styling salon stand today.

Thus, cumulative effects are like biplanes swarming King Kong. One project alone may not carry enough firepower to adversely impact an ecosystem or population. But dozens, hundreds, or thousands of these projects may have enough collective firepower to have a significant lethal impact. The population or ecosystem may hemorrhage, weaken, and tumble to its death.

This cumulation can be hard to see. Sometimes an assessment that determines that a given project will have no significant impacts may be compiled in ignorance, without awareness of previous, current, or future projects that impact the same area. Some may say that this would be as if the four F8C pilots did not know of each other's existence, but the analogy seems to fall apart when one realizes that pilots didn't set out to *wound* Kong, extract some essential bodily fluids, then let him heal up, rather, they intended to *kill* Kong. While our intentions may be subject to debate, the impacts are the same. The object falls to the earth. The Endangered Species Act calls this an "incidental take."[4]

It might be argued that the impacts are hard to see. There are no claw marks on the Empire State Building, no blood on the roof, no bullet casings on the sidewalks, no cracks in the pavement at the intersection of 5th Avenue and West 33rd Street, and no stuffed Kong on display at the Smithsonian, toe tag on his foot. Other than fragile ribbons of cellulite, there is no evidence of the fierce battle that once raged overhead. This is unfortunate. As time passes, the memory of Kong's death slips into unconsciousness while doubts and alternative histories fill the mind.

Stop looking up. In North America, the evidence is piled at our feet: carcasses of Ruby-throated Hummingbird (*Archilochus colubris*), Brown Creeper (*Certhia americana*), Ovenbird, (*Seiurus aurocapilla*), Yellowbellied Sapsucker (*Sphyrapicus varius*), Gray Catbird (*Dumetella carolinensis*), and Black-and-white Warbler (*Mniotilta varia*), Golden-winged Warbler (*Vermivora chrysoptera*), Canada Warbler (*Cardellina canadensis*), Painted Bunting (*Passerina ciris*), Kentucky Warbler (*Geothlypis formosa*), Wormeating Warbler (*Helmitheros vermivorum*), and Wood Thrush (*Hylocichla mustelina*).

Each year, billions of these birds fall to the earth, approaching the number of birds reproduced each year. As with Kong, this is not the work of one assassin's bullet, it's the effect of an armory of weapons. Here are fair or common estimates of the number of birds killed each year in the US in collisions or encounters with various deadly objects:

Communication Towers: 6.8 million birds/year[4]
Vehicles: 89 million birds/year[5]
Buildings: 599 million birds/year[6]
Wind Turbines: 234,000 birds/year[7]
Power Lines: 26 million birds/year[8]
Aircraft: 13,668 in 2014[9, 10]
Domestic cats: 2.4 billion birds/year[11]

The latter figure is controversial. Professor of Anthropology Barbara King complained about "demonizing cats with shaky statistics."[12] This is a very common complaint. While medieval sentiments may inspire superstitious notions about a connection between trembling cats and the netherworld, especially those iniquitous breeds that prowl foggy alleys at night in an icy rain, by and large, these superstitions have been dismissed in our Brain Age. It is well beyond mythology, fable, and anecdote to state that they have an extensive record of stealthy environmental crimes dating all the way back to the Pharaohs, many of whom, by the way, were discovered lying dead alongside their cats.

Red-tailed Hawk.
Steele County, ND, 1998.

Well, this leads us into another protracted debate, this one about our legacy of unintended and unanticipated consequences, that we just can't know every past, present, and future impact around us, nor can we know the sum total of these impacts - a sum that is growing daily and is significantly greater than the sum of its parts - but with a long history of battling beasts to extinction, for all intents and purposes, our beauty is only skin deep.

1. U.S. Office of the Federal Register, Code of Federal Regulations. Cumulative Impacts, 40 CFR 1508.7 (July 1, 2012), https://www.govinfo.gov/app/details/CFR-2012-title40-vol34/CFR-2012-title40-vol34-sec1508-7

2. *King Kong.* Directed by Merian C. Cooper and Ernest B. Schoedsack. United States: RKO Pictures, 1933.

3. T. Longcore, C. Rich, P. Mineau, B. MacDonald, D. G. Bert, et al. "An Estimate of Avian Mortality at Communication Towers in the United States and Canada." *PLoS ONE* 7(4)(2012): e34025. doi:10.1371/journal.pone.0034025

4. U.S. 16 U.S.C. §§1531-1544 (1973).

5. Scott R. Loss, Tom Will, and Peter Marra. "Estimation of bird-vehicle collision mortality on U.S. roads." *The Journal of Wildlife Management* 78 (2014): 763-771.

6. Scott R. Loss, Tom Will, Sara S. Loss, and Peter P. Marra. "Bird–building collisions in the United States: Estimates of annual mortality and species vulnerability." *Condor* 116(1) (2014): 8–23.

7. Scott R. Loss, Tom Will, and Peter P. Marra. "Estimates of bird collision mortality at wind facilities in the contiguous United States." *Biological Conservation* 168 (2013): 201-209.

8. Scott R. Loss, Tom Will, and Peter P. Marra. "Refining Estimates of Bird Collision and Electrocution Mortality at Power Lines in the United States." *PLoS ONE* 9(7) (2014): e101565. doi:10.1371/journal.pone.0101565

9. U.S. Department of Transportation, Federal Aviation Administration, Office of Airport Safety and Standards, *Wildlife strikes to civil aircraft in the United States, 1990-2014*, Richard Dolbeer, Sandra Wright, John Weller, Amy Anderson, and Michael Beiger, Report No. 21, 10.13140/RG.2.1.2370.6649, Washington, DC: U.S. Department of Transportation, 2015.

10. Reza Hedayati and Mojtaba Sadighi, *Bird Strike*. (New York: Woodhead Publishing, 2016).

11. Scott R. Loss, Tom Will and Peter P. Marra. "The impact of free-ranging domestic cats on wildlife of the United States." *Nature Communications* 4.1396 (2014): doi:10.1038/ncomms2380

12. Barbara King, "Do We Really Know That Cats Kill by The Billions? Not So Fast." In NPR (Producer), *Cosmos & Culture, Commentary on Science and Society*, February 3, 2013.

Chapter 18: Point of Failure

There are pleasant distinctions between humans and vegetation. For one, humans do not reproduce vegetatively. Otherwise, Civil War Battlefields would be overrun with children. Nor do we reproduce by achene, berry, pepo, capsule, drupe, follicle, legume, loment, nut, pome, samara, or silique. Otherwise, children would be a crop, subject to drought, insects, and the volatile commodities markets. And humans do not grow out of the remains of other humans. Otherwise, cemeteries would be day-care centers.

However, trees can do all of the above. Some grow vegetatively, they reproduce by a variety of seeds, and they can grow out of the remains of other trees. An old, dead tree lying on the ground that supports the newer trees is called a *Nurse Log*, as in, it nurses the young trees until they can stand on their own. Many old trees started out as young trees growing out of old trees.

The wheel, the pulley, the inclined plane, screw, wedge, lever, these were early machines. In the beginning, they were simple, made of wood, stone, or raw metals. Today, machines are usually elaborate complexes or systems of these simple machines. An example would be a jet engine.

In a system or machine, there are points at which failure can occur. Some points are more prone to failure than others and some points are more critical than others. Some points of failure will stop the entire machine. These are called *Single Points of Failure*. This is an undesirable state; such a machine is highly vulnerable to total system failure. Imagine a jet engine flywheel breaking apart and slicing through the hydraulic lines while cruising at 40,000 feet.

The ideal is to create redundancies, that is, to duplicate critical functions within the machine. That way, if one function fails, a duplicate function takes over and the machine can continue to operate. That is one reason a passenger jet has multiple engines. This is important while traveling eight miles high.

It is also important on the ground. To understand this, we must consider the experience of the mythical *Jedediah Clampett*. According to the legend, when he discovered crude oil on his property in Limestone, Tennessee, it came to the surface under its own power. A small hole punched in the ground by an errant bullet provided relief to the pressurized oil trapped underground. Why, it flowed out of the hole like water from a garden hose and the bubbling crude made old Jed a millionaire.[1]

At that point in time, his machine for oil extraction was no more than a shovel. A shovel is a simple machine, just a wooden handle, a pin, and a blade. It acts as a wedge and lever. Each is a Single Point of Failure. One of those breaks and the tool is useless and Jed is unable to gather any oil. He tosses the handle into the woods, drops to his knees, scoops the oil with a flat rock, and steps back into the Stone Age.

Today, it is unusual to find an oil field that pours from the ground under artesian pressures. Most of the new oil is found at the margins of extractability: in shale, sand, offshore, and deepwater. A shovel will not do. It requires an exceedingly complex machine, a myriad of pipes, valves, gauges, wires, alarms, switches, and sensors. The possible points of failure become innumerable. The Single Points of Failure also increase, requiring a complex arrangement of redundant functions. However, this increases the risk of total system failure and a calamity. In the *Deepwater Horizon* disaster, there were numerous points at which failure occurred - a blowout preventer, two mechanical valves, one battery, one gas alarm, a defective switch, and human oversight - all of which conspired to create a total system failure. Eleven lives were lost, 4.9 million barrels of crude poured into the Gulf of Mexico, and 52,590 tons of mangled metal settled to the bottom of the Gulf.[2] This was just one machine. The planet is littered with millions of broken machines; they are in landfills, backyards, war zones, junkyards, garages, parking lots, sealed in concrete bunkers, ravines, at the bottom of the sea, tumbling in earth orbit. What to do?

A tree is a machine. A large tree functions as a water pump, oxygen generator, carbon sink, weather moderator, fog filter, windbreak, birdhouse, soil stabilizer, food source, to name a few. As with other machines, at some point, it experiences a total system failure, whether it's from drought, insects, lightning, windthrow, climate shift, fungus, landslide, overshading, hydrologic changes. Add them up and there are millions of failure points in a tree. Yet these provide opportunities for other living things. Spring ephemerals take advantage of fall leaf failure and prosper in the abundant spring sunlight. Microorganisms on forest floor take advantage of needle failure and turn them into nutrients. Campers take advantage of branch failure and roast marshmallows. Insects and birds take advantage when the whole tree fails and build

apartments. Other trees take advantage of a fallen tree and drop their seeds into the rotting carcass where they germinate and thrive. Trees grow out of failed trees. This machine is designed to fail.

Fail as they may, we have searched the newspapers and it is very difficult to find accounts of massive explosions, widespread loss of life and limb, or toxic chemical spill associated with the failure of a tree, despite billions of them occurring every year since the late Carboniferous Period.

1. Paul Henning, *The Ballad of Jed Clampett* (Columbia Records, 1962)

2. National Commission on the BP Deepwater Horizon Oil Spill and Offshore Drilling, *Deep Water: The Gulf Oil Disaster and the Future of Offshore Drilling,* Washington, D.C.: GPO, January 2011.

Chapter 19: Minimum Viable Population

Below is an aerial photo showing the distribution of prairie fringed orchid (*Platanthera praeclara*) on 315 acres of tallgrass prairie and wetland on the Sheyenne National Grassland in Ransom County, ND. This is from a 2008 survey. The white dots represent clusters of prairie fringed orchid.

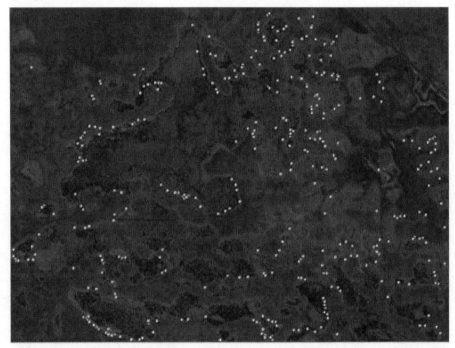

Image: U.S. Geological Survey

This is a federally threatened species. In a given year, there may be 10-20,000 specimens in existence, distributed across 45 counties. This is a drastic decline from pre-settlement populations, which enjoyed vast expanses of tallgrass prairie habitat. Today, that habitat is one of the rarest in North America.

While 10-20,000 plants in 45 counties may sound like a lot, it is not. Here is why: As mentioned earlier, species have what are called

Minimum Viable Populations (MVP), or extinction thresholds. These are population numbers below which they spiral into extinction. Below this threshold, the effects of inbreeding, loss of genetic variability, or loss of mating opportunities are fatal to the population. They go extinct.

There have been attempts to establish a universal MVP. In the 1980's it was suggested that at least 50 individuals were needed to prevent inbreeding and 500 individuals were needed to prevent genetic drift.[1] Genetic drift is the change in frequency of a particular gene variant, which can be devastating if that frequency is a decline or loss of frequency. Which is to say, a loss of genetic diversity, a capacity to express traits that may be needed in a given environment. This is called a shrinking gene pool.

But those threshold numbers, while somewhat useful, are persistently impractical because reproductive rates, existing genetic diversity, and habitat requirements vary from species to species. Consider: Those of us who have been ushered into the Space Age are aware that we are now able to look back at ourselves from a distant vantage point. A nighttime view from 223 miles above the earth shows the arrangement of human populations, bright, lighted clusters of humans with dark, somewhat depopulated gaps in between. This satellite view is of the state of Nebraska, in the middle of North America.

Image: USGS/NASA Landsat

As you may have noticed, the populations of *Platanthera praeclara*, and in fact, most other species, are arranged in a similar way. Rather than being evenly or regularly distributed across the landscape, populations are usually clustered in nodes or centers with gaps of relatively unpopulated land in between. The entire network of lights or population clusters in a given region may be likened to a metapopulation. The arrangement of clusters is largely driven by habitat suitability. For humans, that is rivers, fertile valleys, groundwater, wind protection, trails, coffee shops, casinos, taverns.

Removing a population cluster removes their genetic material from the metapopulation. This may be insignificant if there are enough individuals remaining in the metapopulation that contain the same genetic material. But removing many more populations will increase the risk that vital genetic material is removed (or recessive genes are expressed) from the entire metapopulation. Thus, most people

understand that the total number of species must be maintained at a high level.

However, here is where the total numbers can mislead, as in 10-20,000 orchids or 370 black-footed ferrets or 25,000 Red Knots. Back to the satellite photo. Suppose the metapopulation in the photo is 20,000 people. What would happen if all of those remaining populations were cut off from one another, if you removed the corridors between populations, the roads, rivers, railroads, and air routes? The breeding population would be reduced to the population of the city, in this scenario, maybe no more than 1000 people. The population would become like the inhabitants of a walled city surrounded by siege engines. This forces consanguineous marriage, prohibits the exchange of genetic material with outside populations, creating a community much like the royal families of ancient times. Gigantic jaws, cartoon character hands, flowerpot-shaped heads. In this scenario, the effective population is not the metapopulation, it is the individual population cluster. They are restricted to their own shallow, stagnant gene pool, sluggish, in a torpor, each generation less fit than the last. As the catapults fling blighted cattle over the walls, the inhabitants of the besieged city succumb to plague, infertility, reproductive failure, and loss of mates. Extinction approaches on fused feet.

The lesson? This teaches us that it is not enough to consider total population numbers, it is necessary to consider the *access* one subpopulation has to another. This means corridors - suitable habitat patches connecting populations - are essential in maintaining an MVP.

In the end, the niches are filled, the city is reinhabited, and soon there is a bustling metropolis teeming with cane toads, mongoose, brown tree snakes, Norway rats, Asian carp, feral pigs, water hyacinth, and a broad spectrum of strip malls. At the moment, humans appear to have the genetic diversity needed to adapt to these threats. In the meantime, however, the orchids, ferrets, and Knots cannot interpret aerial photography; they have no idea what approaches their city walls.

1. M. L. Shaffer, "Minimum population sizes for species conservation," *BioScience* 31 (2) (1981): 131–134.

Chapter 20: Alien Invasive Species

Alien invasive species (AIS) are organisms that are introduced into a foreign ecosystem, usually at a great distance from their native ecosystem, usually from another continent. That's the alien part. The invasive part is that they rapidly invade, populate, and exclude other species in the new territory. Some may refer to them as exotic species. Some may refer to them as noxious weeds, but some noxious weeds are native plants that have been branded as undesirable because of economics, cultural norms, or ignorance.

Why the fuss? - after all, they are just plants.

It is like this: A kid on holiday goes overseas and picks up a microbe. Easy enough to do. But he has no immunity to this one; his immune system has never seen it before. He returns home and goes back to school. He starts to cough. Next, all the kids start to cough. Then the teachers start to cough. The principal gets a cough. Nobody has immunity to the microbe, and it runs amok. So, the school sends everybody home and locks the doors. Quarantine. Police tape. Face masks. At home, their bodies work long and hard to develop an adequate immune response. But some immune systems are not strong, fast, or educated enough. The microbe wins. The body loses. Enough losses and the school is shut down for good.

It's this way with AIS. Introduce a foreign organism into an ecosystem and there may be no defense against it, in this case, no predators, parasites, weather patterns that would check its advance, weaken or kill it. So, it runs amok. If it continues to dominate and exclude the native species, the original ecosystem may be damaged, no longer be recognizable, or it may be gone for good.

Get out of my spot.

A prime example of this is salt cedar, or tamarisk (*Tamarix* sp.), brought to North America from the Middle East in the 1800's, which has invaded riparian areas in the American southwest, making the native southwestern riparian area one of the rarest ecosystems in the US. Guns, bombs, napalm won't stop it. It's a phreatophyte, driving roots to extreme depths to take up water, so much so, that they may be consuming millions of acre-feet of water per year, enough to supply millions of people for one year. Other threatened ecosystems are northeastern forests (garlic mustard), southern waterways (water hyacinth, nutria), Great Lakes (gobi, zebra mussel, Asian carp), southeastern forests (Kudzu), Yellowstone Lake (lake trout), glaciated northern forests (alien invasive earthworms (yes)). It's a long list.

But AIS aren't always plants, mammals, birds, fish, reptiles, and insects; lately, we have come to know it can involve tiny species invisible to the naked eye. That kid who went overseas and suffered badly wasn't eaten by an escaped lion. So too, ecosystems can be brought to the brink by alien, invasive microbes. You may be familiar with some of these in North America: Dutch Elm Disease (American elm), Whirling Disease (trout and salmon), White-nose Syndrome (bats), and Viral Hemorrhagic Septicemia (fish).

And then there is *Didymosphenia geminata*, known as Didymo, an AIS diatomic algae expanding and bullying its way through clear streams around the world - North America, Australia, Argentina, Chile, New Zealand. Some researchers believe that it was introduced to some areas on the soles of waders worn by globe-trotting trout fishermen. But others believe that it is native to North America and Europe and has become more abundant in its original habitat in recent years. A 2014 study concluded that it was native in eastern Canada and proposed that its "blooms likely form in response to regional consequences of climate warming, rather than human introduction."[1]

Other alien life forms have been created in laboratories right here on earth. A recent engineering marvel is transgenic herbicide-resistant creeping bentgrass (*Agrostis stolonifera* L.). The species and its transgene are spreading unintentionally by seed and by pollen in the northeastern United States and it hybridizes with a dozen other *Agrostis* and *Polypogon* species.[2,3] It had been bioengineered to resist a widely used herbicide. Its turf growth habit made it suitable for golf courses. Thus, this grass could be easily maintained through herbicide application, creating a thick monoculture of creeping bentgrass, free of all other plant life, a weed-free zone, the ideal golf course. Picture rolling fairways from sea to shining sea.

A query of the literature does not produce a single study of native golf course ecosystems anywhere on earth anytime in the past four hundred thousand years, including pollen core studies, although, given enough time, the golf course ecosystem would be classified as a naturalized ecosystem, and given even more time, this ecosystem would be the only ecosystem on earth, aside from landfills and drug resistant bacteria colonies.

There are many lessons in this. A foreign organism that is relocated apart from its antagonists, the predators, parasites, and other checks against its advance, is poised to dominate an ecosystem. Ecosystems set back to early seral stages are open for invasion. Anthropogenic climate change can promote invasive populations.

Yet, some folks think that all the fuss about AIS is unfounded, reasoning that nature has been moving species around for eons, that everything is a non-native species at one time or another, and there is no need to worry, the earth accommodates them all. True, but as mentioned in Chapter 8, we are moving hundreds of millions of airline passengers at hundreds of miles per hour and hundreds of millions of those metal shipping containers across the oceans every year. This is way beyond the background species migration rate. It must be asked, if this is no big deal, do the folks who dismiss this as fearmongering get vaccinated before they travel overseas?

1. J. M. Lavery, J. Kurek, K. M. Rühland, C. A. Gillis, M.F.J. Pisaric, J. P. Smola, "Exploring the environmental context of recent Didymosphenia geminata proliferation in Gaspésie, Quebec, using paleolimnology," *Canadian Journal of Fisheries and Aquatic Sciences*, 71(4) (2014): 616-626, https://doi.org/10.1139/cjfas-2013-0442

2. Lidia S. Watrud, E. Henry Lee, Anne Fairbrother, Connie Burdick, Jay R. Reichman, Mike Bollman, Marjorie Storm, George King, and Peter K. Van de Water, "Evidence for Landscape-level, Pollen-mediated Gene Flow from Genetically Modified Creeping Bentgrass with CP4 EPSPS as a Marker," *PNAS* Volume 101 (40) (2004): 14533-38.

3. Jay R. Reichman, Lidia S. Waltrud, E. Henry Lee, Connie A. Burdick, Mike A. Bollman, Marjorie J. Storm, George A. King, and Carol Mallory-Smith, "Establishment of transgenic herbicide-resistant creeping bentgrass (Agrostis stolonifera L.) in nonagronomic habitats," *Molecular Ecology* 15 (2006), 4243-4255

Chapter 21: Carbon Fingerprint

Decaying blocks of coal are washed up on the banks of the Missouri River in western North Dakota. This coal is from a geologic stratum called the Sentinel Butte Formation. Lignite is a soft, brownish coal with fewer calories and more moisture than other coals, making it an intermediary between peat and bituminous or anthracite coal. The Sentinel Butte Formation is from the late Paleocene Epoch in the early Cenozoic Era. This epoch began after the K-Pg extinction event, which marked the extinction of dinosaurs and the advent of mammals. It is old.

It has been observed that that plains Indians did not burn much of this coal, nor did the Corps of Discovery as they sailed by these bluffs two hundred years ago. It was on July 28, 1806 that William Clark observed that the coal was of "inferior quality".[1] Their fuel of choice was firewood cut from the cottonwood, ash, elm, and juniper trees that were plentiful along the Missouri River. This is for good reason. The smokes of hickory, mesquite, apple, alder, cherry and other woods have long been popular flavorings in grilled foods, but we have yet to see any food products on the market that advertise "Natural Coal Smoke Flavor", nor do we expect to see any in the near future. A century later, the hapless homesteaders did make use of the lignite, perhaps out of the desperation of the times, and by 1939, at the height of the Great Depression, there were some 309 mines operating in North Dakota. But today there are only six coal mines out there and two of those produce oxidized lignite, not for burning. None for food.

The distinction between coal smoke and wood smoke goes beyond successful backyard barbeques. While coal and wood both originate as plant matter and terminate as fuel, the antiquity of the plant matter accounts for a significant difference in the chemistry of the fuel, a distinct carbon fingerprint. Here is how it works: Humans have a symbiotic relationship with plants. We produce carbon dioxide as waste matter, plants consume carbon dioxide as food. Carbon comes in about 15 sizes, called isotopes. Three are naturally found on earth: ^{12}C, ^{13}C, and ^{14}C. The latter is a radioactive isotope, unstable, formed by cosmic radiation, ultimately decaying into an isotope of Nitrogen. This is a slow deterioration; the half-life of ^{14}C is 5,730 years.

Lignite on the shore of the Missouri River in western North Dakota.

While living, a plant incorporates atmospheric carbon in its tissues. The balance of carbon isotopes in its tissues reflects the balance of carbon isotopes in the atmosphere. When a plant dies, it no longer takes in carbon and the carbon that remains in its tissues is fixed, set. From this point, the unstable ^{14}C continues to decay, slowly depleting the dead tissues of ^{14}C.

In the short term, what this means is, when a dead cottonwood limb is thrown into a campfire, and the wind shifts and casts the plume of campfire smoke over the campers, they are inhaling smoke almost fully stocked with busy, buzzing, radioactive ^{14}C atoms. Only a few atoms have been lost to decay. However, when a chunk of Paleocene coal is thrown into a campfire, and the wind shifts and the smoke descends upon the ashen, hacking campers, they inhale a lighter, more decadent smoke, one depleted of ^{14}C atoms.

In the mid-term, the empirical evidence is there has been a dramatic increase in carbon in the earth's atmosphere. Currently, we are above 400 ppm. That's a 100% increase since the ice age and a level 25% higher than anything for the past 400,000 years. Where is all that carbon coming from?

The answer is in the chemistry of the carbon. The atmospheric carbon, while increasing in quantity, has been steadily decreasing in

^{14}C in the past century; it is being *depleted* of ^{14}C, something known as the "Suess Effect".[2] This could not be from the burning of firewood or rain forests, grassland or forest fires, or burning other plant matter of recent origin. These would produce smoke that has nearly the full stock of ^{14}C, which would not deplete the atmosphere of ^{14}C. This must be from the combustion of carbon sources that are depleted in ^{14}C - ancient plant matter has lost its ^{14}C through radioactive decay. Their combustion products lack ^{14}C and thereby deplete the atmosphere of ^{14}C. This is the source of the increased carbon. This is what is called "fossil fuel." Coal, natural gas, petroleum. Old plant matter.

Ah, the smoking gun.

In the long-term, it is estimated that there are over one trillion tons of extractable coal reserves on earth, which would last 150 years at present consumption rates. At the same time, combustion of these reserves in that time frame would contribute to a novel set of environmental conditions on earth. As Gavin Foster states:

> Humanity's fossil-fuel use, if unabated, risks taking us, by the middle of the twenty-first century, to values of CO_2 not seen since the early Eocene...If CO_2 continues to rise further into the twenty-third century, then the associated large increase in radiative forcing, and how the Earth system would respond, would likely be without geological precedent in the last half a billion years.[3]

Without precedent. At which point, *all* trees may be ancient plant matter, food may grill spontaneously, coal-flavored dishes may be standard fare, and visibility would be reduced to the foot of one's hospital bed. Let us cough. Welcome to our remodeled, planetary home. Let's rename it *Hell.*

1. M. Lewis, W. Clark, and Members of the Corps of Discovery, *The Original Journals of the Lewis and Clark Expedition 1804-1806, Volume 5* (Reuben Gold Thwaites, Ed.) (New York: Dodd, Mead, and Company, 1905), 305.

2. Charles D. Keeling, "The Suess effect: ^{13}Carbon-^{14}Carbon interrelations." *Environment International,* Vol. 2 (1979): 229-300.

3. Gavin Foster, et al. "Future climate forcing potentially without precedent in the last 420 million years." *Nature Communications*, Vol. 8 (14845) (2017)

Chapter 22: Altered Stream Flow

A few decades ago, there was some debate about the number of words for snow used by inhabitants of the Arctic regions. Some said that Eskimos had one hundred words for snow. This would not be a surprise, were it to be true. In English, there are many words for frozen precipitation: snow, sleet, hail, rime. There are three kinds of lava: pahoehoe, aa, and pillow. There are numerous kinds of wetlands: swamp, bog, fen, marsh, shrub-carr, peatland. Our natural world becomes subdivided. Sometimes this can be exploited. At one time there were just a few types of chocolates available, now there are thousands. Almond chocolate, sea-salt chocolate, orange chocolate, mushroom chocolate, beef-flavored chocolate, chocolate sauerkraut, and so forth. The point is, once a person studies something for a few years, that person begins to see distinctions between what had at one time been considered identical objects. This is what perception does to us.

It is the same with fish: They can be salt-water, fresh water, benthic, pelagic. Benthic: at the lowest level of a body of water. Pelagic: at the upper layers of a body of water. Their eggs have distinctions, too. They can be buoyant or can sink. Their buoyancy varies based on "egg specific gravities that tune the egg buoyancy to create specific vertical distributions for each local population".[1] What that means is, the eggs are designed to linger in a water level that is optimum for their development. For some, that's suspended at a particular level in the water column, others are at or near the bottom. Some eggs are adhesive, sticking to objects in the water, often in the benthic zone. Some eggs come in masses and others are single. So, we have variables of adhesiveness, buoyancy, and mass. There are other variations, like fish who lay their eggs on beaches or mud, fish that build nests, fish that are mouth brooders and this is quickly getting out of hand and we are running out of words.

This is the story: Around the world, many species of fish are disappearing. Some of these are from the mid-continental rivers and streams in North America. Here is a list of six imperiled fish species from these waters:

Rio Grande Silvery Minnow (*Hybognathus amarus*) – Endangered
Bluntnose Shiner (*Notropis simus*) – Endangered
Arkansas River Shiner (*Notropis girardi*) – Threatened
Rio Grande Shiner (*Notropis jemzanus*) – Near-threatened
Plains Minnow (*Hybognathus placitus*) – Numerous but in serious decline
Speckled Chub (*Macrhybopsis aestivalis*) – Substantial long-term decline

There are other species in the same waterways that are not currently imperiled. Why is this?

What the six imperiled species have in common is each one of them produces non-adhesive, semi-buoyant eggs. They are members of what is called a "semi-buoyant egg reproductive guild." The buoyancy is sufficient to suspend the egg in turbulent or flowing waters of rivers. It is in this buoyant, pelagic state that the egg develops to maturity. Were the eggs of these species to sink to the bottom, they would settle into sediment and die. This is to say that the eggs are dependent upon a river current for success. How much river current?

The eggs take 1-2 days to hatch and the newly hatched larvae must be in suspension for several more days where they "swim up" and develop their gas bladder and absorb their yolk sac. Thus, as they are developing, the eggs and larvae depend upon a current that can keep

126

them in suspension for 3-5 days. Being carried for 3-5 days in a current will transport the eggs a distance downstream that depends upon the flow rate of the river. A conservative drift rate of 3 km/hour would transport the eggs "72-144 km before hatching. Developing protolarvae could be transported an additional 216 km during the swim-up stage".[2] Thus, the eggs and larvae would need a total of 288-360 km or 179-224 miles of contiguous moving water.

Therein lies the answer. When dams were placed along the rivers that these species inhabited- Upper Pecos, Middle Pecos, Middle Rio Grande, Arkansas - they often broke the length of free-flowing river into segments less than 179 miles. Long stretches of the river are now behind impoundments and there, the water is nearly still. Any semi-buoyant, non-adhesive eggs that enter the impoundment will stall out, sink down through the pelagic zone to the benthic zone, settle into the sediment, and die. Other alterations in natural stream flow patterns have also thwarted the reproductive success of these species. It is no surprise then, that fish with non-buoyant and adhesive eggs, those that are successful in the benthic zone, thrive.

Every day brings something new. What is *this*? We are looking for a simple phrase that describes the relentless alteration of natural habitats through semi-permanent, short-sighted, and ill-conceived schemes that randomly endanger species in an offhand way, but we are lost for words.

1. Svein Sundby and Trond Kristiansen, "The Principles of Buoyancy in Marine Fish Eggs and Their Vertical Distributions across the World Oceans," *PLoS One*, Vol. 10(10) (2015): 1

2. Steven P. Platania and Christopher S. Altenbach, "Reproductive Strategies and Egg Types of Seven Rio Grande Basin Cyprinids," *Copeia*, Vol. 1998(3) (1998): 566.

Chapter 23: Quarantine

On August 12, 1775, the Spanish naval officer Juan de Ayala named an island in San Francisco Bay after the California Brown Pelicans (*Pelecanus occidentalis californicusis*) that were common in the bay. The archaic Spanish word for Pelican is "Alcatraz." This is fitting. In 1827, a French captain wrote that the island was "covered with a countless number" of pelicans.[1] Of greater interest though, was the strategic position of the island. In 1850, the President reserved the island as a military installation, barbette guns were installed, and in 1858, it was converted into a military garrison. The isolation, inaccessibility, and cold waters surrounding the island were seen as attributes suitable for a prison and in 1861, the island was used to house Civil War prisoners. It was designated as a long-term detention center in 1868, a military prison in 1907, and a Federal prison in 1934. So isolated, impenetrable, and inaccessible was the prison that only three men were ever able to escape - three professionally trained actors at that - an event captured on film on a Panavision Panaflex color camera in 1.85 to 1 ratio and shown to millions of shaken viewers in 1979.[2] However, all of the pelicans escaped and were never caught. They no longer nest on the island.

Good move. Ordinarily, barriers are constructed to keep certain objects from mixing with other objects. For a variety of reasons, right or wrong, someone sees a need for separation, whether it is phosphorus and water, tourists and lava, employees and management, audience and truth, road salt and roads, astronauts and absolute zero, or John Anglin and society at large.

We have two trends. At one time, there were *natural* barriers on earth, things like oceans, mountain ranges, rivers, climate zones, ice fields, and deserts. These kept certain living things from mixing, living things on one side of the barrier that had traits that threatened the existence of living things on the other side of the barrier. As discussed earlier, these barriers have been penetrated by motorized aluminum and steel cylinders, wonders of long distance, high-speed travel. Once on the other side, we behave like liberating armies, releasing wildlife into new lands, not realizing that we behave more like the doomed armies of Troy, who unwittingly transported a wooden horse filled with enemy soldiers through the gates of their fair city. A night of mad celebration ensued, followed by deep sleep. The soldiers poured out of the horse and massacred the inhabitants of Troy.

Anglin seed from Alcatraz Island. NPS Photo, public domain.

At this time, we have *artificial* barriers. These have been constructed for a variety of reasons. Some have been erected to slow the advance of invading armies of non-native species. A prime example is the system of electric barriers set across the bottom of the ever-popular Chicago Sanitary and Ship Canal (CSSC), whose creamy, mossy-grey waters glisten in the brown sunlight that beams through the photochemical smog, "a river and canal system running so thick with fecal coliform that signs along the banks warn that the contents below are not suitable for 'any human body contact.'"[3] These have been installed with the intent of preventing the migration of non-native, aggressive bighead, silver, and black carp into the Great Lakes, where they would devastate the current fishery, which had replaced a previously devastated fishery, which had replaced a previously devastated fishery, which had replaced a previously devastated - the barrier goes both ways; it is also intended to prevent the species that devastated the Great Lakes - tubenose goby, ruffe, sea lamprey - from entering the Mississippi River system and devastating the current fishery, which had replaced a previously devastated fishery, which had.

How many layers of which had are in this story, anyhow? The next layer is probably a tale of a new species of electric carp that makes sailors jump off of their ships into the coliform-rich water where they are cooked alive.

Doesn't say dead or alive.
Photo: Paul Benda.

Another fine example is a silt fence. The earthmoving associated with the construction of objects along water bodies such as the CSSC - that *Civil Engineering Monument of the Millennium*, that *National Historic Place* - is isolated, that is to say, *quarantined* by a silt fence, a plastic mesh barrier that is designed to capture the debris that would be carried away by rainfall or snowmelt into the water body. Along the CSSC, this would include the occasional mobster.

Similar objectives lie behind the construction of sound barriers along highways. Over 3,000 miles of these barriers have been erected in the US, which has 164,000 miles of highway. Traffic produces noise from engines, aerodynamics, and tires slapping on pavement, typically 70 to 80 decibels, about the sound of a roaring blender held at arm's length. Artificial, sustained noise at these levels has adverse impacts on wildlife, including loss of hearing, inability to detect environmental cues, increased heart rate and respiration, and altered behavior, including site abandonment and failed reproduction. Similar effects are seen in humans. Adaptive responses in humans are usually limited to behavioral changes such as increased and sustained personal noise production and sonic and interpersonal isolation. For economic reasons, many humans in such environments are entrapped like animals caged in a zoo, having impaired migratory ability.

On the foggy night of September 13, 2013, seven-thousand-five-hundred migrating songbirds burned to death in a gas flare at a liquefied natural gas receiving and regasification terminal in Saint John, New Brunswick. The dead birds included Red-eyed Vireos, Parulas, Black-and-white Warblers, Magnolia Warblers Redstarts, thrushes, Rose-breasted Grosbeaks, and possibly Olive-sided Flycatchers and Canada Warblers.[4] Many birds migrate at night and, like insects, are attracted to light, even hot light. Once they are lured by lights into urban or suburban settings, many remain in the habitat-poor environment, where they experience increased mortality. Into the den of cats, they fly. This is a windfall to the American suburban housecat population, which, under the cover of darkness and out of sight of humans, quietly dispatches about 2.4 billion birds each year. That cat sneaking across the kitchen counter while your back is turned is probably turning on the porch lights, those new LEDs, the ones designed to save something.

Humans are affected as well. Aside from disrupted sleep patterns, one-third of the human race is unable to see the night sky; the glow of a city is visible on the horizon anywhere in the northeastern U.S. To reduce the spillage of these man-made photons into the environment - steadily increasing as humans switch over to LED lighting - shields are installed on streetlights and some skyscrapers shut off their lights at night.

Numerous other examples could be described here, such as clay liners beneath landfills, armed patrols around wildlife refuges, earthen berms around large aboveground petroleum storage tanks. Each is an example where human activity is segregated from the natural environment, an implicit recognition of the damaging effects that these common activities and/or their byproducts have upon the ecosystem.

An inspection of petroleum tanks, landfills, wildlife refuges, streetlights, highways, and earthmoving projects around the planet reveals that the vast majority of these lack protective barriers. We are at large. The wise animals don't wait to be moved to zoos or preserves or other protective custody; they are in self-imposed exile. The unfortunate ones are trapped by forces beyond their control and their continued existence is in question as they lose hearing, fail to recognize dangers, alter their behavior, and fail to reproduce.

Alcatraz was closed on March 21, 1963. But wildlife can't tell the difference between a prison and a shopping mall and all the while, the fence surrounding our territory is expanding across the globe. Given enough time, all of our territories would merge, becoming a global institution. There would be no natural environment to shield from us. We are like a wooden horse filled with silt, unrecycled plastic, deafening noise, a million lumens, leaking petroleum, and we have passed through the gate, we have crossed the border. Certainly, this may be with all good intent, but whatever it is, they are afraid of Humans, even those bearing gifts.

1. Auguste Duhaut-Cilly, *A Voyage to California, the Sandwich Islands, and Around the World in the Years 1826–1829* (Oakland, CA: University of California Press, 1999), 284.

2. *Escape from Alcatraz*, Directed by Don Siegel. United States: Paramount Pictures, 1979.

3. Julia Apland Hitz, "Chicago Sanitary Canals, Anything but Sanitary." *State of the Planet* (blog). Earth Institute, Columbia University. July 12, 2010. blogs.ei.columbia.edu/2010/07/12/chicago-sanitary-canals-anything-but-sanitary/

4. "7,500 Songbirds Killed at Gas Plant in Saint John," CBC news, CBC/Radio Canada online, September 18, 2013. www.cbc.ca/news/canada/new-brunswick/7-500-songbirds-killed-at-canaport-gas-plant-in-saint-john-1.1857615.

Chapter 24: Demanufacture

In recent years, astronomers have been tracking what are called Near Earth Objects. Occasionally, they announce that an object such as an asteroid is coming dangerously close to the earth. What purpose this warning serves is unclear. It might be that they want us all to brace for impact - crawl under a desk, curl up, and put our hands behind our heads.

This is nothing new. Judging by the accumulated testimony of hundreds of science fiction writers in the past century, aliens have either approached or landed on earth hundreds of times. Yet, the human race has survived all of these encounters and continues to thrive, showing vigorous signs of life; eating, drinking, replicating, gaming, fighting, and sleeping.

However, not many have considered what sort of impact this would have had on any aliens that would have landed on this forbidden planet. Odds are it would have been traumatic. But, contrary to the contentions of these authors, this trauma would not be due to 1) a lack of immunity to bacterial infection, 2) intolerance to high-frequency sound, 3) the caustic effects of water, 4) a weakness in the directed-energy weapon port, which, when destroyed, causes a devastating chain reaction, destroying the entire mothership,[1] or 5) extreme cranial pressure when hearing Slim Whitman's *Indian Love Call*.[2]

From 250 miles up in space, if aliens approached the dark side of the earth, they might see the array of amber lights in urban zones and highways and remark at how beautiful they seem. Upon landing on

Lake Michigan, they might see the Chicago skyline a half-mile away, reflected in the water, and wax poetic about the splendor of the tall concrete and steel structures with mirrored walls.

By night the skyscraper looms in the smoke and the stars and has a soul.[3]

Breaking into the third floor of an office building, they would marvel at the landscape architect's drawings depicting the clean, crisp, sunny, aesthetic contours of an exclusive suburban subdivision. Underground service maps would show a beautifully organized web of fiber optic cables, telephone lines, electrical lines, drinking water lines, natural gas lines, storm sewers, sanitary sewers, and steam pipes. No wonder they want to invade this place.

As discussed in Chapter 10, an increasing percentage of nature photography is framed such that it doesn't include the telephone poles, highways, contrails, discarded plastic bottles, discarded tires or abandoned refrigerators. Some photographers erase the offending sights with photo editing software. So it is with the architectural drawings and maps.

That plastic bottle just out of view in that award-winning nature photo, that photo on display at the art institute just down the street from those aliens, well, consider the engineering that went into it. We proudly present the process that brings us *polyethylene terephthalate*: Obtain some crude oil. Using heat, distill the crude oil. One of the fractions is naphtha. Catalytically reform the naphtha, producing benzene, toluene, and xylene. Distill the xylene, separating p-xylene from m-xylene, o-xylene, and ethylbenzene. Next, oxidize the p-xylene with atmospheric oxygen using cobalt–manganese–bromide catalyst, which produces terephthalic acid. Combine ethylene glycol with the terephthalic acid, producing a polymeric chain of polyethylene terephthalate molecules. Then cut into pellets and stretch-blow them into plastic drinking bottles at rates of 500 to 10,000 bottles per hour with a stretch blow molding machine. Next, take that bottle and toss it into the ditch. That's right, toss it. This is what is called "end use", in this case, its final use is as a chemical and physical threat to all life on earth.

This forces nature photographers to narrow their field of view, producing increasingly narrow images of the world. This skews our estimation of what is actually out there in the natural world. This is the same distorted perspective that the alien is experiencing as he views our earth from 250 miles, or from one-half mile away at night, or on cheerful architectural drawings.

Daylight arrives all too soon, and the sun shines on creeks, estuaries, bays, shorelines, and whirling gyres teeming with plastics, plastic-eating fish and birds, plastic microfibers in beer, plastic microbeads in the streams and lakes, and plastic microfibers floating in the air.[4] The aliens may be having second thoughts.

Yet, over time, this bottle may appear to disappear. Not so. Although the polyethylene terephthalate polymer degrades with considerable effort by the sun, the atmosphere, and the climate, it releases toxic chemicals along the way and the individual plastic molecule is extremely durable and persists indefinitely. John Hahladakis states:

> The majority of plastic polymer types are non-biodegradable, i.e. degradation by microorganisms, where PET and PP being the most abundant ones, are practically non-degradable...However, a complete conversion of a plastic material to its main constituents (CO_2, water and inorganic molecules) via photo- and bio-degradation is rather unlikely to happen.[5]

Fortunately, or maybe not, invisibility is not an issue with the majority of human constructs. A closer inspection of the landscape that surrounds the de-polymerizing bottle in the ditch shows degrading man-made structures, from underground utility infrastructures to highways, bridges, high-rises, houses, landfills, and industry, including that aging, inefficient recycling plant that is leaking something vile into the river, each of which produces a unique set of toxins and voluminous waste. This did not show up on the beautiful, four-color, urban planning maps.

That big highway full of truck-eating potholes, one may recall a time when a four-lane highway was just a side street. Or when there were no traffic lights a town that now has dozens. Growth in population and standard of living result in increased infrastructure. Given enough time, every highway would be at least four-lane and every intersection on earth would have a traffic light. There are tens of thousands of landfills in the US and probably hundreds of thousands of landfills, official and informal, around the world. Given enough time, every square foot of the earth would be a former or existing landfill. The next level of solutions would be similar to those used in cemeteries or cities, or is it cities or cemeteries, where land is scarce: Put on a second story. High-rise landfills.

It is difficult to find pre-industrial age debris. Decaying infrastructure from centuries past was composed of wood, metal, cloth, bone, stone, glass. Decomposition of these reduced the majority of it to sand, carbon dioxide, water, or inorganic molecules. Other materials were often recycled, used for new houses, bridges, walls. Often, what remains to this day seems to be part of the natural landscape, something organic, an aesthetic match to the surroundings.

Depositos de Pinkuylluna,
500-year old Inca granaries
Ollantaytambo, Peru, 2019

Somewhere in the past 200 years, we lost the art and science of an organic life, biodegradable products, low impact, native building materials, of constructs that appeared to be part of the natural landscape. A law of nature is, what is constructed must be integrated, biologically, chemically, and physically to the natural environment. Look around, bird nests, beaver lodges, termite hills, hornet nests, and muskrat lodges. It would follow that whatever we make should be in accord with the biology, ecology, chemistry, and visuals of life. Many of our constructs are better suited for the surface of Venus, where temperatures are 462 degrees and it rains sulfuric acid. A law of nature is, everything produced must be *de-manufactured*. It would follow that whatever we make we should be responsible to *unmake*. But the moment our products leave the laboratory, they become orphans, abandoned on the steps of nature. Somehow, we find ourselves way above the law.

Meanwhile, those aliens. In broad daylight, they take a closer look. They see plastic packaging as ubiquitous as dandelions. And there are those potholes in the pavement, the delaminating OSB, leaking drums of chemical waste, crumbling tarpaper shingles, rusting rebar, worn carpet, discarded faux leather couches, warped vinyl siding, oxidized paint, junk cars, leaking oil pipelines, this growing mound of stubborn, toxic waste. They flee to their mothership, screaming.

Aliens, they say, we can't defeat them.

One more thing, make that 6) repelled by our trash.

1. *Independence Day*. Directed by Roland Emmerich. United States: Centropolis Entertainment, 1996.

2. *Mars Attacks!* Directed by Tim Burton. United States: Tim Burton Production Company/Warner Brothers, 1996.

3. Carl Sandberg, *Chicago Poems* (New York: Henry Holt and Company, 1919).

4. Steve Allen, Deonie Allen, Vernon R. Phoenix, Gaël Le Roux, Pilar Durántez Jiménez, Anaëlle Simonneau, Stéphane Binet & Didier Galop. "Atmospheric transport and deposition of microplastics in a remote mountain catchment." *Nature Geoscience,* 12 (2019), 339–344.

4. John N. Hahladakis, Costas A. Velisa, Roland Weber, Eleni Iacovidou, Phil Purnell, "An overview of chemical additives present in plastics: Migration, release, fate and environmental impact during their use, disposal and recycling," *Journal of Hazardous Materials*, 344 (2018): 184

Chapter 25: Global Recovery

Time machines, now those would have a huge market. Imagine if there were two models running simultaneously. Imagine how hard it would be to plan anything.

There have been many turning points in collective history where a minor deviation in a course of events would have resulted in a drastically different future. If only the Donner Party had not taken Hastings Cutoff. If only Archduke Ferdinand's driver had heard about the changed motorcade route. If Emperor Atahualpa and his soldiers had not been unarmed when they met Pizarro in Cajamarca. This is true on a personal scale as well. If only we hadn't joined the circus, married that securities broker, eaten that food from the street vendor. Things would have been different.

Unfortunately, avoiding Hastings Cutoff would have sparked an altogether new history, a chain of events that could have gone in any direction. Who knows, it could have culminated in a two-dimensional world dominated by flattened entertainment figures where reading and writing did not exist. That's hard to imagine.

This prediction comes to us courtesy of the thing called the *Multiverse*, popular in some corners of physics and science fiction. Multiverse, as in multiple universes. The theory proposes that infinite, bubble, mathematical, and daughter multiverses exist. The theory is that, in a variety of respects, an infinite number of universes are possible. For one, it is said that an infinite range of possible effects of a single decision exists, each existing in one of an infinite number of universes. Currently, we are looking for the universe where none of that is true and nobody believes it.

The problem is, these days, science fiction and science are often confused. It is easy for some to confuse theory with evidence. A strong theory may be cited as *evidence* for the existence of the particulars of the theory. For example, someone may say, "There is strong evidence of a multiverse", in view of the persuasive argument, logic, and math describing the theory. But that isn't evidence. Evidence would be an observation, an object, a mark from that universe. It is understandable how people could be confused. Today, many will quickly jump from possibility to belief because of the weight assigned by disinformation salesmen and their clientele to insubstantial and improbable claims. It is becoming normal for many to believe in that which is unbelievable.

Well, it is said that nature does not like a vacuum. This may explain why, when the compulsion to misbehave is greater than the will to change, rationalizations quickly fill the void. Several types are commonly found in the void: Deny the misbehavior occurred, shift the blame for the misbehavior, and minimize the gravity of the misbehavior. *Who me? You made me do it. Well, everybody else does it.*

So here is the moral inventory: In our relationship with the natural environment, we act too quickly to extract too much natural resource to build things too big and too complex, doing so with limited knowledge and cognition amidst increasing disinformation, which, in turn, suppresses and replaces native ecosystems, increases failure points, pushes species below minimum population thresholds, distributes alien invasive species, increases atmospheric carbon, alters stream ecology, resulting in the loss of species and habitats, herds, flocks, schools, and we don't have the time for yet another doggone list.

As we are confronted with the evidence of our incapacitated escapades from the centuries before, the environmental misdeeds, the temptation is to deny the facts and the need to change our behavior and thought. That sound of rushing air is the sound of a rationalization filling the void. *We didn't do it; extinction is part of nature. We were just following orders; industry and government told us to do it. Well, at least we didn't kill all the bison.* Lately, it has been, *Don't worry, science will find a way to clean up our mess.*

Keep tossing the plastic bottles out the window, someone is out there picking them up. And there are multiple universes out there, spinning like a million samaras falling from a maple tree, where the all the right decisions were made. And in the future, science will make a time machine where we can go back and make amends with history, to turn the Donner Party to the north on the California Trail, inform Ferdinand's driver to continue driving along Appel Quay, and get Atahualpa skip the meeting in Cajamarca and go rally his troops, to make sure plastic was contained in the laboratory, the mixed-grass prairie was never plowed, the diversion of the Amu Darya and Syr Darya that feed the Aral Sea was never conceived, the Saint Lawrence Seaway was scrapped, the Ogallala aquifer was conserved, and Oppenheimer was a simple shoe salesman, all of which would, of course, create more multiverses that don't exist. And besides, the natural outcome of evolution is self-extermination. As one sinks deeper into maladjustment, the rationalizations become more delusional, beliefs become more magical. There is a bottom to this, somewhere, it just depends if one falls long and far enough to feel it.

Raising the floor.
Dr Strangelove, Columbia Pictures.
Public Domain.

By now, the ground should be getting awfully close. This is about this time that our life should flash before our eyes, Ah, so many regrets. It's painful to think about - but that's nothing like the pain that awaits a hundred feet below. The biggest regret may that we lost our understanding that just because something *could* exist does not mean

143

it *does* exist. It is entertaining to fantasize about time travel, going back and forth in history altering the calamitous decisions, as is done on a regular basis in the film studios in Hollywood by ageless actors and actresses who obviously are benefitting from the time-slowing effects of traveling at the speed of light, but the common citizen does not have the luxury of committing a consequential series of decisions spanning centuries that result in environmental catastrophes and walking off the set to the comfort of climate control and personal bodyguards. It would be better to let the fantasies exist in the secure confines of the film studio, behind high walls, limited access gates guarded by armed security personnel, and boom barriers. Don't let them out.

Well, it's about time for our friends to intervene. The rationalizations don't work anymore. There is no time machine to go back and do it all over. No alternative universe where we made the right decisions. Ah, if we could do it over again, things would have been different. No, better yet, do *us* all over again.

That's more like it. Next time we get a planet, let's do it right.

THE END

Bibliography

US GOVERNMENT PUBLICATIONS

Hubbard, Henry V. "The Designer in National Parks" in *National Park Service, 1941 Yearbook: Park and Recreation Progress.* Washington, DC: US Government Printing Office, 1941.

U.S. Census Bureau, *Current Population Survey, Annual Social and Economic Supplements, 1940 and 1947 to 2018* (2018), https://www.census.gov/programs-surveys/saipe/guidance/model-input-data/cpsasec.html

U.S. Department of Commerce, *2017 Characteristics of New Housing* (2018), https://www.census.gov/construction/chars/

U.S. Department of Energy, Los Alamos National Laboratory, *'Where is everybody?" An account of Fermi's question*, by Eric M. Jones, Report No: LA-10311-MS, 1981) doi:10.2172/5746675.

U.S. Department of Transportation, Federal Aviation Administration, Office of Airport Safety and Standards, *Wildlife strikes to civil aircraft in the United States, 1990-2014*, Richard Dolbeer, Sandra Wright, John Weller, Amy Anderson, and Michael Beiger, Report No. 21, 10.13140/RG.2.1.2370.6649, Washington, DC: U.S. Department of Transportation, 2015.

U.S. Fish and Wildlife Service, *Endangered Species Facts. Piping Plover* [Fact sheet] (2001).

U.S. Office of the Federal Register, Code of Federal Regulations. Cumulative Impacts, 40 CFR 1508.7 (July 1, 2012), https://www.govinfo.gov/app/details/CFR-2012-title40-vol34/CFR-2012-title40-vol34-sec1508-7

U.S. 16 U.S.C. §§1531-1544 (1973).

BOOKS, JOURNALS, REPORTS, ARTICLES, ETC.

Alcoholics Anonymous, *Questions & Answers on Sponsorship.* New York: Alcoholics Anonymous World Services, Inc., 1983.

Allen, Steve, Deonie Allen, Vernon R. Phoenix, Gaël Le Roux, Pilar Durántez Jiménez, Anaëlle Simonneau, Stéphane Binet & Didier Galop. "Atmospheric transport and deposition of microplastics in a remote mountain catchment." *Nature Geoscience*, 12 (2019), 339–344.

Arnett, Peter. "Major Describes Move." *New York Times,* February 8, 1968.

Berkeley, George. *A Treatise Concerning the Principles of Human Knowledge.* Philadelphia: J. B. Lippincott and Co., 1874.

Bornmann, Lutz and Ruediger Mutz. "Growth rates of modern science: A bibliometric analysis based on the number of publications and cited references." *Journal of the Association for Information Science and Technology,* 66(11 (2015).

Cave, Tamasin and Andy Rowell. *A Quiet Word: Lobbying, Crony Capitalism and Broken Politics in Britain.* New York: Random House, 2014.

Collins, Michael D. "Putative audio recordings of the Ivory-billed Woodpecker (Campephilus principalis).".*J. Acoust. Soc. Am.* 129(3) (December 2010).

Darwin, Charles. *On the Origin of Species.* Cambridge, MA: Harvard University Press, 1859.

Dragland, Åse. "Big Data, for better or worse: 90% of world's data generated over last two years." SINTEF, Trondheim, Norway, May 22, 2013, https://www.sintef.no/en/latest-news/big-data-for-better-or-worse/

Duhaut-Cilly, Auguste. *A Voyage to California, the Sandwich Islands, and Around the World in the Years 1826–1829.* Oakland, CA: University of California Press, 1999.

Dunbar, R. I. M. (1992). "Neocortex size as a constraint on group size in primates". *Journal of Human Evolution.* 22 (6): 469–493.

Editorial Team. "The Exponential Growth of Data." Inside Big Data, February 16, 2016, https://insidebigdata.com/2017/02/16/the-exponential-growth-of-data

Farnham, Thomas J. *Travels in the Great Western Prairies, the Anahuac and Rocky Mountains, and in the Oregon Territory.* Poughkeepsie NY: Killey & Lossing, 1841.

Flood, Theodore L. "The Editor's Table." *The Chautauquan,* June 1883, Volume III, No. 9.

Foster, Gavin, et al. "Future climate forcing potentially without precedent in the last 420 million years." *Nature Communications,* Vol. 8 (14845) (2017).

Fryxell, John M., Anna Mosser, Anthony R. E. Sinclair, and Craig Packer. "Group formation stabilizes predator–prey dynamics." *Nature,* 449 (2007).

Hahladakis, John N., Costas A. Velisa, Roland Weber, Eleni Iacovidou, Phil Purnell. "An overview of chemical additives present in plastics: Migration, release, fate and environmental impact during their use, disposal and recycling." *Journal of Hazardous Materials,* 344 (2018): 184

Hammerstein, Oscar II. *The Farmer and The Cowman.* Williamson Music Company, 1955.

Hanson, Robin. *The Great Filter — Are We Almost Past It?* 1998. Accessed October 14, 2019, http://mason.gmu.edu/~rhanson/greatfilter.html

Hart, Albert Bushnell. *Formation of the Union, 1750-1829.* New York: Longmans, 1892.

Hedayati, Reza and Mojtaba Sadighi; *Bird Strike.* New York: Woodhead Publishing 2016.

Henning, Paul. *The Ballad of Jed Clampett.* Columbia Records, 1962.

Hitz, Julia Apland. "Chicago Sanitary Canals, Anything but Sanitary." *State of the Planet* (blog). Earth Institute, Columbia University. July 12, 2010. blogs.ei.columbia.edu/2010/07/12/chicago-sanitary-canals-anything-but-sanitary/

Horace. 33BCE. *Satires. Satire VIII.*

IPBES, *Summary for policymakers of the global assessment report on biodiversity and ecosystem services of the Intergovernmental Science-Policy Platform on Biodiversity and Ecosystem Services.* S. Díaz, J. Settele, E. S. Brondizio E.S., H. T. Ngo, M. Guèze, J. Agard, A. Arneth, P. Balvanera, K. A. Brauman, S. H. M. Butchart, K. M. A. Chan, L. A. Garibaldi, K. Ichii, J. Liu, S. M. Subramanian, G. F. Midgley, P. Miloslavich, Z. Molnár, D. Obura, A. Pfaff, S. Polasky, A. Purvis, J. Razzaque, B. Reyers, R. Roy Chowdhury, Y. J. Shin, I. J. Visseren-Hamakers, K. J. Willis, and C. N. Zayas (eds.) (Bonn, Germany, IPBES secretariat, 2019)

Keeling, Charles D. "The Suess effect: ^{13}Carbon-^{14}Carbon interrelations." *Environment International,* Vol. 2 (1979): 229-300.

King, Barbara. "Do We Really Know That Cats Kill by The Billions? Not So Fast." In NPR (Producer), *Cosmos & Culture, Commentary on Science and Society,* February 3, 2013.

Kirk, Paul. *Crime Investigation. Physical Evidence and the Police Laboratory.* New York: Interscience Publishers, Inc., 1953.

Kujit, Ian. "People and Space in Early Agricultural Villages: Exploring Daily Lives, Community Size, and Architecture in the Late Pre-Pottery Neolithic." *Journal of Anthropological Archaeology* 19(1) (2000): 75–102.

Lanciani, Roldolfo A. *Ancient Rome in the light of recent discoveries.* Cambridge, MA: The Riverside Press, 1888.

Langford, Nathaniel P. *Vigilante Days and Ways.* Boston: J. G. Cupples Co., 1890.

Lavery, J. M., J. Kurek, K. M. Rühland, C. A. Gillis, M.F.J. Pisaric, J. P. Smola. "Exploring the environmental context of recent Didymosphenia geminata proliferation in Gaspésie, Quebec, using paleolimnology." *Canadian Journal of Fisheries and Aquatic Sciences* 71(4) (2014): 616-626, https://doi.org/10.1139/cjfas-2013-0442

Leopold, Aldo. *A Sand County Almanac and Sketches Here and There.* New York: Oxford, 1949.

Lewis, M., W. Clark, and Members of the Corps of Discovery. *The Journals of the Lewis and Clark Expedition, Volume 3 August 25, 1804-April 6, 1805.* (G. Moulton, Ed.). Lincoln, NE: University of Nebraska Press, 2002.

Lewis, M., W. Clark, and Members of the Corps of Discovery. *The Original Journals of the Lewis and Clark Expedition 1804-1806, Volume 5* (Reuben Gold Thwaites, Ed.). New York: Dodd, Mead, and Company, 1905.

Locard, Edmond. *La police et les méthodes scientifiques.* Paris, Éditions Rieder, 1934.

Longcore, Travis, Catherine Rich, Pierre Mineau, Beau MacDonald, Daniel G. Bert, Lauren M. Sullivan, Erin Mutrie, Sidney A. Gauthreaux Jr, Michael L. Avery, Robert L. Crawford, Albert M. Manville II, Emilie R. Travis, David Drake. "An Estimate of Avian Mortality at Communication Towers in the United States and Canada." *PLoS ONE* 7(4) (2014): e34025. doi:10.1371/journal.pone.0034025

Loss, Scott, Tom Will, and Peter Marra. "Estimation of bird-vehicle collision mortality on U.S. roads." *The Journal of Wildlife Management* 78 (2014): 763-771.

Loss, Scott R., Tom Will, Sara S. Loss, and Peter P. Marra. "Bird–building collisions in the United States: Estimates of annual mortality and species vulnerability." *Condor* 116(1) (2014): 8–23.

Loss, Scott R, Tom Will, and Peter P. Marra. "Estimates of bird collision mortality at wind facilities in the contiguous United States." *Biological Conservation* 168 (2013): 201-209.

Loss, Scott R., Tom Will, and Peter P. Marra. "Refining Estimates of Bird Collision and Electrocution Mortality at Power Lines in the United States." *PLoS ONE* 9(7) (2014): e101565. doi:10.1371/journal.pone.0101565

Loss, Scott R., Tom Will and Peter P. Marra. "The impact of free-ranging domestic cats on wildlife of the United States." *Nature Communications* 4.1396 (2014): doi:10.1038/ncomms2380

Powell, Roger A. and Michael S. Mitchell. "What is a home range?", *Journal of Mammalogy* 93(4) (2012): 948–958.

Mandelbrot, Benoit. "How Long Is the Coast of Britain? Statistical Self-Similarity and Fractional Dimension." *Science* 156(3775) (1967), 636

McLelland, Linda Flint. *Building the National Parks: Historic Landscape Design and Construction.* Baltimore, MD: The John Hopkins University Press, 1998.

Millington, R. M. *A Rhythmical Translation of the First Book of the Satires of Horace. Longman's.* London: Green, Reader, and Dyer, 1869.

Monteith, Kevin L., Ryan A. Long, Vernon C. Bleich, James R. Heffelfinger, Paul R. Krausman, and R. Terry Bowyer. "Effects of harvest, culture, and climate on trends in size of horn-like structures in trophy ungulates," *Wildlife Monographs* 183(1) (2013). doi:10.1002/wmon.1007

Musgrave, Ruth S., Sara Parker, and Miriam Wolok. "The Status of Poaching in the United States - Are We Protecting Our Wildlife?", *Natural Resources Journal* 33(4) (1993).

National Commission on the BP Deepwater Horizon Oil Spill and Offshore Drilling, *Deep Water: The Gulf Oil Disaster and the Future of Offshore Drilling,* Washington, D.C.: GPO, January 2011.

Nettle, Daniel Nettle, Mhairi A. Gibson, David W. Lawson, and Rebecca Sear. "Human behavioral ecology: current research and future prospects." *Behavioral Ecology* Volume 24(1) (September 2013): 1031–1040

Nemeth, Irwin and Henrik Brumm. "Birds and Anthropogenic Noise: Are Urban Songs Adaptive?" *Am Nat.* 176(4) (October 2010): 465-75

Ohler, Norman. *Blitzed - Drugs in the Third Reich.* Boston, MA: Houghton Mifflin Harcourt, 2017.

Olden, Julian D., Julie L. Lockwood, and Catherine L. Parr. "Biological Invasions and the Homogenization of Faunas and Floras" in *Conservation Biogeography*, ed. Richard J. Ladle and Robert J. Whittaker. West Sussex UK: Wiley-Blackwell, 2011. DOI:10.1002/9781444390001

Olmstead, Frederick Law Jr. "The Distinction between National Parks and National Forests." *Landscape Architecture* 6 (3) (1916): 115, 116.

Olmstead, Frederick Law Jr. "Vacation in the National Parks and Forests." *Landscape Architecture* 12 (2) (1922): 108.

Pimentel, David. "Ethanol Fuels: Energy Balance, Economics, and Environmental Impacts Are Negative." *Natural Resources Research* 12(2) (2003): 127–134

Platania, Steven P. and Christopher S. Altenbach. "Reproductive Strategies and Egg Types of Seven Rio Grande Basin Cyprinids." *Copeia* Vol. 1998(3) (1998): 566.

Pover, Todd and Christina Davis. "Piping Plover Nesting Results in New Jersey: 2015." Conserve Wildlife Foundation of New Jersey. Retrieved from http://www.conservewildlifenj.org/downloads/cwnj_658.pdf

Reston, James. "The Flies That Captured the Flypaper." *New York Times,* February 7, 1968.

Rathje, William L. *Rubbish! The Archaeology of Garbage.* New York: Harper Collins, 1992.

"Red China: Death to Sparrows." *Time Magazine*, May 5, 1959.

Reichman, Jay R., Lidia S. Waltrud, E. Henry Lee, Connie A. Burdick, Mike A. Bollman, Marjorie J. Storm, George A. King, and Carol Mallory-Smith, "Establishment of transgenic herbicide-resistant creeping bentgrass (Agrostis stolonifera L.) in nonagronomic habitats," *Molecular Ecology* 15 (2006), 4243–4255

Sandberg, Carl. *Chicago Poems.* New York: Henry Holt and Company, 1919.

Sanderson, Eric W., Redford, Kent H., Weber, Bill, Aune, Keith, Baldes, Dick, Berger, Joel, Carter, Dave, Curtin, Charles, Derr, James, Dobrott, Steve, Fearn, Eva,

Fleener, Craig, Forrest, Steve, Gerlach, Craig, Gates, C. Cormack, Gross, John E., Gogan, Peter, Grassel, Shaun, Hilty, Jody A., and Jensen, Marv. "The Ecological Future of the North American Bison: Conceiving Long-Term, Large-Scale Conservation of Wildlife." *Conservation Biology* 22(2) (2008): 252-266.

Schueneman, Tom. "Scientist on Western Hudson Bay Polar Bear Population: 'I Consider Myself a Historian.'" PlanetWatch, March 10, 2008, https://earthmaven.io/planetwatch/biodiversity/scientist-on-western-hudson-bay-polar-bear-population-i-consider-myself-a-historian-eG-fssfST0eig-54SdvAPg/

Shaffer, M. L. "Minimum population sizes for species conservation." *BioScience* 31 (2) (1981): 131–134.

Sibley, David Allen. *National Audubon Society, The Sibley Guide to Birds.* New York: Alfred A. Knopf, 2000.

Sikkink, Pamela G. "Yellowstone Sage Belts 1958 to 2008: 50 Years of Change in the Big Sagebrush (Artemisia tridentata) Communities of Yellowstone National Park." *Natural Resources and Environmental Issues* 17(19) (2011).

Slater, John G. *The Collected Papers of Bertrand Russell, Vol. 11: Last Philosophical Testament, 1943–68.* Abington: Routledge, 1983.

Stokes, Donald and Lillian Stokes. *Stokes Field Guide to Birds. Western Region.* New York: Little, Brown, and Company, 1996.

Sulzer, David, Mark S. Sonders, Nathan W. Poulsen, and Aurelio Galli. "Mechanisms of neurotransmitter release by amphetamines: A review." *Progress in Neurobiology* 75 (2005): 406–433.

Sundby, Svein and Trond Kristiansen. "The Principles of Buoyancy in Marine Fish Eggs and Their Vertical Distributions across the World Oceans." *PLoS One* Vol. 10(10) (2015): 1

Van Noorden, Richard. "Global scientific output doubles every nine years." Nature Newsblog, May 7, 2014, http://blogs.nature.com/news/2014/05/global-scientific-output-doubles-every-nine-years.html

Venema, Vibeke. "When time stood still. A Hiroshima survivor's story." *BBC News*, July 24, 2010, http://www.bbc.co.uk/news/special/2014/newsspec_8079/index.html

Watrud, Lidia S., E. Henry Lee, Anne Fairbrother, Connie Burdick, Jay R. Reichman, Mike Bollman, Marjorie Storm, George King, and Peter K. Van de Water, "Evidence for Landscape-level, Pollen-mediated Gene Flow from Genetically Modified Creeping Bentgrass with CP4 EPSPS as a Marker." *PNAS* Volume 101 (40) (2004): 14533-38.

Weber, Max. *Essays in Sociology*, trans. H. H. Gerth and C. Wright Mills. New York: Oxford University Press, 1946.

Weckend, Stephanie, Andreas Wade, Garvin Heath. "End-of-Life Management: Solar Photovoltaic Panels." International Renewable Energy Agency (IRENA) and

International Energy Agency Photovoltaic Power Systems (IEA-PVPS), Report Number: T12-06:2016, June 2016.

Wikipedia, The Free Encyclopedia, s.v. "The Attack of the 50 Foot Woman." (Accessed April 15, 2019), https://en.wikipedia.org/wiki/Attack_of_the_50_Foot_Woman

Wilcox, Bruce A. and Dennis D. Murphy. "Conservation Strategy: The Effects of Fragmentation on Extinction." *The American Naturalist,* Vol. 125(6) (June 1985), 879-887

Winship, George P., *Coronado's journey to New Mexico and the great plains* (New York: A. Lovell, 1894), 580.

1. World Economic Forum, *The New Plastics Economy — Rethinking the future of plastics* (Ellen MacArthur Foundation and McKinsey & Company, 2016), http://www.ellenmacarthurfoundation.org/publications

Wright, Frank Lloyd. *An Autobiography.* New York: Duell, Sloan, and Pearce, 1943, 146.

WWF. "Living Planet Report 2016. Risk and resilience in a new era." Gland, Switzerland: WWF International, 2016, http://awsassets.panda.org/downloads/lpr_2016_full_report_low_res.pdf

"7,500 Songbirds Killed at Gas Plant in Saint John," CBC news, CBC/Radio Canada online, September 18, 2013. www.cbc.ca/news/canada/new-brunswick/7-500-songbirds-killed-at-canaport-gas-plant-in-saint-john-1.1857615.

MOVIES

Dizzy Pilots. Directed by Jules White. United States: Columbia Pictures, 1943.

Escape from Alcatraz, Directed by Don Siegel. United States: Paramount Pictures, 1979.

Independence Day. Directed by Roland Emmerich. United States: Centropolis Entertainment, 1996.

Invasion of The Body Snatchers. Directed by Don Siegel. United States: Walter Wanger Productions. 1956.

King Kong. Directed by Merian C. Cooper and Ernest B. Schoedsack. United States: RKO Pictures, 1933.

Mars Attacks! Directed by Tim Burton. United States: Tim Burton Production Company/Warner Brothers, 1996.

North by Northwest. Directed by Alfred Hitchcock. United States: Metro-Goldwyn-Mayer, 1959.

Oklahoma! Directed by Fred Zinneman. United States: Rodgers & Hammerstein Pictures, 1955.

The Amazing Colossal Man. Directed by Bert I. Gordon. United States: American International Pictures, 1957.

The Attack of the 50 Foot Woman. Directed by Nathan Juran. United States: Woolner Brothers Pictures Inc., 1958.

The Curse of the Fly. Directed by Don Sharp. United States: 20th Century Fox, 1965.

The Fly. Directed by Kurt Neumann. United States: 20th Century Fox, 1957.

The Incredible Shrinking Man. Directed by Jack Arnold. United States: Universal Pictures, 1957.

The Thing from Another World. Directed by Christian Nyby. United States: Winchester Pictures Corporation, 1951.

Them. Directed by Gordon Douglas. United States: Warner Brothers, 1954.

Made in the USA
Columbia, SC
21 October 2020